THE ✦ TEEN
SPELL
BOOK

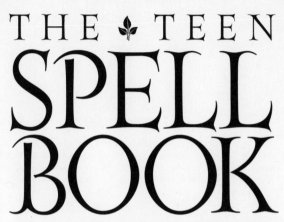

THE ✦ TEEN SPELL BOOK

Magick for Young Witches

Jamie Wood

Celestial Arts
Berkeley / Toronto

A Kirsty Melville Book

Celestial Arts
P.O. Box 7123
Berkeley, California 94707
www.tenspeed.com

Distributed in Australia by Simon and Schuster Australia,
in Canada by Ten Speed Press Canada, in New Zealand by Southern Publishers Group,
in South Africa by Real Books, in Southeast Asia by Berkeley Books, and in the United
Kingdom and Europe by Airlift Book Company.

Cover and interior design by Jeff Puda

Library of Congress Cataloging-in-Publication Data

Wood, Jamie.
The teen spell book: magick for young witches/Jamie Wood
p.cm.
"A Kirsty Melville Book"—T.p. verso.
Includes Bibliographical references and index.
Summary: A volume of spells and Wiccan lore, including such spells as "Contact
someone who has died," "Getting your crush to fall for you," and "Make colleges beg
for you."
ISBN 1-58761-115-5 (alk. paper)
1. Magic—Juvenile literature 2. Charms—Juvenile literature 3. Witchcraft—Juvenile
literature [1. Charms. 2. Magic. 3. Witchcraft.] I. Title.
BF1611 .W85 2001
133.4'3—dc21
2001037163
First printing, 2001

Printed in Canada

2 3 4 5 6 7 8 9 10—05 04 03 02 01

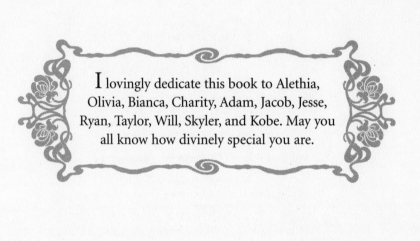

I lovingly dedicate this book to Alethia, Olivia, Bianca, Charity, Adam, Jacob, Jesse, Ryan, Taylor, Will, Skyler, and Kobe. May you all know how divinely special you are.

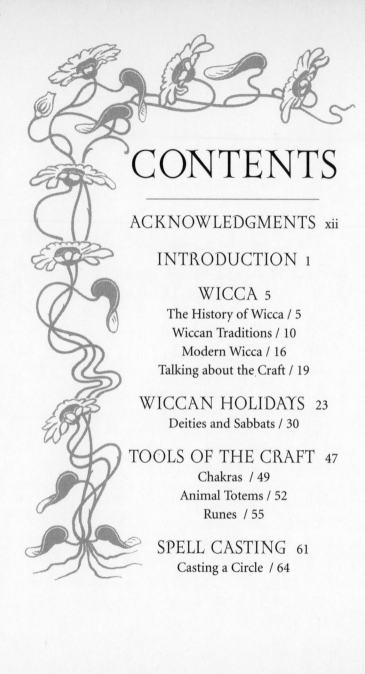

CONTENTS

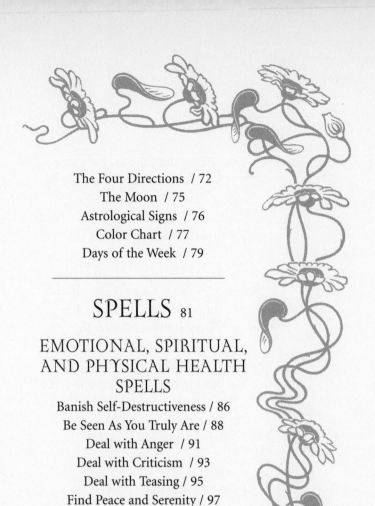

SPELLS 81

EMOTIONAL, SPIRITUAL, AND PHYSICAL HEALTH SPELLS

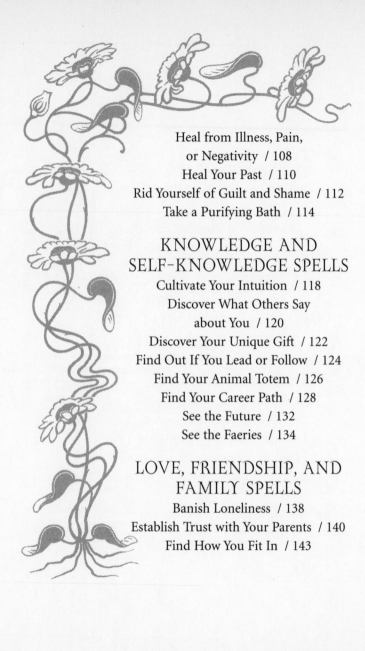

MONEY SPELLS

PROBLEM-SOLVING SPELLS

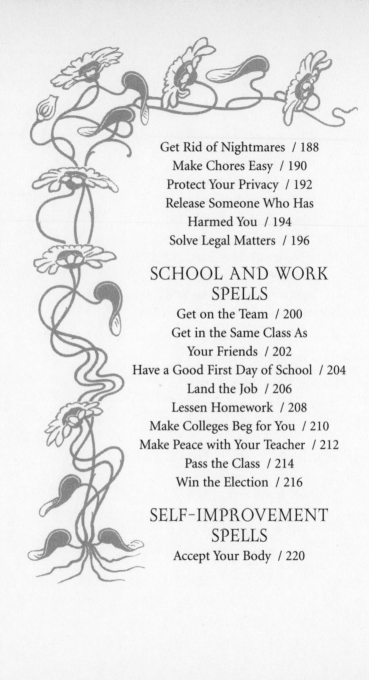

SCHOOL AND WORK SPELLS

SELF-IMPROVEMENT SPELLS

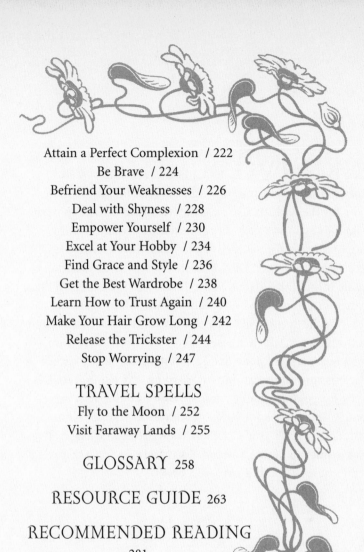

ACKNOWLEDGMENTS

I want to thank my family, lovingly guided and protected by Kevin, for their patience during the writing and creation of this book; I love you so much. My gratitude goes out to Danny, Sean, Brannen, Elise, Cheryl, Cheri, Chrystie, Mel, Amy, Jen, Mara, Dawn, Summer, Don, Marléné, Jane, C.J., Crystal, Julia, Megan, Mom, Dad, Elaine, Mary, Tara, Page, Katie, and Andreas for their inspiration and confidence in me. Many thanks to Katherine, Ruth, and Nila for helping me clear the channel and discard the pain, which allowed me to write this book from a strong heart center. Many thanks to Victoria Bearden for her sagacious rune information. Thank you to my editor, Windy Ferges, for your availability, guidance, and kindness; to my agent, Julie Castiglia, for your encouragement, support, and fortitude; my sixth-grade teacher, Ms. Kneece, who saw it all and stood by me; and Carla Foster for watching, loving, and caring for my babies so I could write this book.

INTRODUCTION

s a young girl, I relentlessly pursued every whim, dream, or desire that crossed the movie screen of my mind. I knew no fear. I believed in angels and Spirit guides—and that I had a host of them on my side: I was invincible. In time I excitedly tried to share my experiences with others. But it was as if I was speaking another language when I talked about miracles of nature or Spirit's profound impact on my life; people called me weird and shut me out. I felt hurt and alone, like I was in a black hole. I began to give my power away by looking outside for acceptance. I followed the natural human tendency to want to fit in and tried to conform to "normality." Even though I was the same person, I had lost my grounding and self-confidence.

I felt like I did not belong, that my people were somewhere else—like the ugly duckling or Stellaluna. The pressure became great as I went after my dreams, and instead of moving full—steam ahead, I tentatively looked around, waiting for others' sidelong glances, comments, and judgments. I often changed according to their responses, and in the process lost a bit of my individuality. I was angered and scared by my willingness to change.

One afternoon alone at home, I began to listen to the small still voice inside. It was as if a promise of so much more was *still* available, and I was not living the life I was meant to live.

I began to appreciate time alone and the calm, soothing voice, not the criticizing one screaming at me to change or rebel—breaking the boundaries that kept me safe.

I am not saying it is not okay to push the limitations once and a while. The challenging nature of teenagers is what keeps society from falling asleep, conforming into one mind, and living a mundane life. I was to risk, but the risk I am talking about pertains to a willingness to be who I was meant to be—a beloved and proud child of Spirit.

In time my intuition grew, and I found that coincidences happened all the time. With concentration, I could foresee events in my life and in the lives of those close to me. I found that with deliberate focus, my true needs were met easily and effortlessly, though these were not always the wants and appearances I thought the coolest.

I began to be aware that nurturing my childlike innocence and enthusiasm was important if I was to maintain this connection. The childlike, symbolic, right-brained, mystical mind believes in Santa Claus, faeries, the Easter Bunny, ghosts, and miracles.

I recall the first time I heard Spirit tell me to stay innocent and free of guilt or shame. I was in sixth grade on the playground. It was a whisper from behind my right shoulder: *Remember: Remember who you truly are—the Goddess, God incarnate, in the flesh. You are unique and outside of any mold, and that is just as it should be.*

I believe everything happens for a reason, and my path was just what should have been. How do I know? Because that is the way it happened. There have been times when I wished I had the courage in my teen years to constantly apply my secretive knowledge of my Divine nature to my everyday living. Now, I want to impress on you to not give up—continue to exercise this oneness with Spirit. As I enter the mother phase of the Goddess, I hope to reach out and help you up. Or I can simply be here for you on your path—present, nonjudgmental, with acceptance of your unique expression and journey.

As a girl, you represent the maiden or princess. When you reach puberty or age fifteen, as a young woman you become the enchantress. You are captivating, charming, and delightful: full of light and magick. As a boy, you are the lad and embody a curious nature. When you reach puberty or age fifteen, as a young man you become the adventurer or warrior. You are a symbol of daring, courage, protection, and the provider. Together you represent innocence, possibilities, purity, vulnerability, and quietness before rising to your full and unique expression.

It can be difficult to be a lone light in a world in which most others find it easier to shroud themselves in darkness; but do not give up. So many of us light bearers are coming out of the darkness. You are not alone.

Sisters and brothers, you are the torchbearers, bringing the light of awareness to the forefront of society. You possess the talent and ability to make all your dreams come true. The honor of keeping the lore of these ancient wise teachings alive, while balancing and harmonizing male and female energy, rests on your capable shoulders. You have the power. You *are* power.

WICCA

icca is a gentle, earth-based religion that follows and celebrates the rhythm of nature. Followers abide by the Wiccan Redes: Do What Thou Will As Long As You Harm None and Whatever You Do Comes Back To You Three Times Three Times Three (known as the Threefold Law). Modern Wicca is an eclectic collection of life-honoring pathways that can be tailored to your unique individual needs and desires or practiced with a coven under a specific tradition. The meaningful customs and celebrations of Wicca are steeped in a rich history that reaches deep into ancient matriarchal societies.

THE HISTORY OF WICCA

Earth-based religions, including Wicca, predate Christianity, Judaism, Buddhism, and Hinduism. Relics, cave drawings, and more evidence of the worship of nature date back more than thirty-five thousand years. Ancient followers honored the two forces: the male God of the hunt, symbolizing death and rebirth and the essence of the fields and forests; and the female Goddess of fertility, creation, and the birth giver. Divinity or Spirit, the one source (whichever you choose to call it), is a combination of the balance of these two energies. These ancestors celebrated the natural forces, cycles of the seasons, and life with ritual, song, and personal attunement with Spirit.

One of the last times the majority of people lived closely with the land occurred during the Middle Ages (approximately 400–1475 A.D.). Then, people had to follow the cycles of the seasons to survive. They paid attention to signs, omens, and the premonitions offered by nature and the spirit world. They did not try to interpret everything through their logical brains. Their days were filled with mystery and symbolism.

Everyone believed witches existed and had a certain amount of power over the supernatural world. Most people used magick, potions, spells, charms, and the like. The supernatural permeated the medieval world, and the boundaries between the natural physical world and the metaphysical spiritual world were very thin. Most people believed there were people who could control the unseen forces of the supernatural world; this was magick. It took the actions of the church to convince most people that the devil was involved.

Churchmen in the late Middle Ages and early modern period came to believe that anyone who used any kind of magick *must* be working with the devil. To many churchmen, magick users were a threat to the authority of the church. Magick users could seemingly manipulate the unseen forces in ways that churchmen thought only God should be able to do. The church was not comfortable with magick or witches for this reason and because magick often was associated with older, pre-Christian traditions, which still had a strong hold on the minds and hearts of the common folk. Churchmen worked hard to convince the common folk that magick users, specifically those that used their magick to do harm, were in fact agents of the devil.

It is important to remember, though, that there is *no* proof (by modern standards) that anyone burned in the witch-hunts was actually in league with the devil. Another misconception about the witch-hunts has also been corrected. Historians have shown that few, if any, midwives were burned as witches. In fact, because of their medical knowledge and especially their intimate knowledge of the female body, midwives often worked for the authorities in their pursuit of witches. As medical professionals, they performed the physical search of the accused witch's body.

Historians argue about the reasons for the dramatic increase in witch trials and burnings in the mid-1500s. Many historians argue that rapid changes in the economy, society, religion, and politics all made for a very stressful time. For hundreds of years, there had been only one church—the Universal Catholic Church—but then many different forms of Christianity arose. Sometimes villages were split into rival religious groups. In all countries the way the economy worked changed drastically as capitalistic ideas and market forces changed the way people did business. As if this were not enough, the economic changes created new social groups that demanded political influence. The traditional organization of society and traditional social relationships, in which everyone knew their place in the hierarchy, shifted to support the new social organization. Instead of being influenced and controlled by the local lord, the national government, headed by the king, had the power.

This all happened at virtually the same time! On top of it all, the world continued to suffer from the plague and a variety of other diseases. Very little medical knowledge could actually relieve most human suffering. Wars brought on by all the religious and economic change laid large areas of Europe to waste, making the suffering even greater. The people wanted a scapegoat, someone to blame all their problems on.

With the rise of Christianity's power, many Wiccan followers began to practice secretly. They used code words or phrases such as *eye of newt, dragon's blood,* or *lizard tongue* to disguise the healing and ceremonial herbs and rituals. They used symbols to represent ideas of their religion, such as the triple moon, which represents the three faces of the Goddess. These symbols were engraved into chalices, sewed on robes, or marked on their doors. All this was done to keep their lore, traditions, and practices alive, as well as themselves.

People continued to be burned for one hundred years because of the age-old fears of the devil combined with the economic, religious, political, and social stresses of the time. Who was behind it all? Some argue that the church (both Protestant and Catholic) drove the witch craze out of fear that the devil, hoping to bring about the end of the world, was abroad in the world and causing all the hardships and suffering. Churchmen believed in a great conspiracy between witches and the devil.

The governments went along with the churchmen out of fear of the chaos the devil would bring about. This is known as the "top-down" theory of the witch craze.

Other historians argue that the churchmen and the governments were only responding to the fears and demands of the common folk to rid the world of witches. Life in a village was not the community ideal we like to think it was. In a world with no social security checks, no welfare, no public hospitals, and so on, you had to rely on your neighbor for survival—this did not mean you had to like your neighbor, or even trust him or her all the time. In such a world, given the right opportunity, especially in times of great change and stress, villagers turned on one another—accusing one another of witchcraft. During the sixteenth and seventeenth centuries, the common folk found plenty of reasons to accuse their neighbors, because so much change and hardship had happened. This is the "bottom-up" theory of the witch craze.

So what is the answer? Well, it is most likely that the true story is somewhere in the middle of these two theories. The common folk could not kill off so many witches without help from the elite (churchmen and nobility). Before the witch craze, everybody believed witches existed and had a certain amount of power over the supernatural world; they just did not see them as such a big threat. However, under the right circumstances, the fears of the common folk combined with the intellectual ideas about the devil, magick, and authority created a society ready and willing to not only accuse a bunch of people of evil witchcraft, but also burn them (perhaps thirty to sixty thousand people burned).

It was not until the early to mid-1900s that brave souls such as Isaac Bonewits, Gerald Gardner, Charles Godfrey Leland, Margaret Murray, Doreen Valiente, Patricia Crowther, Stewart Farrar, and Raymond Buckland came out of the broom closet to openly speak about the Wiccan religion and its teachings. Their writings and those of modern authors and teachers such as Scott Cunningham, Margot Adler, Raven Grimassi, and Starhawk are noted on page 281 in Recommended Reading.

WICCAN TRADITIONS

There are many traditions and ways of practicing Wicca—from Faerie, to Gardnerian, Dianic, Italian, Celtic, Egyptian, and Norse. Although the approach to attain spiritual connection with the Divine will differ within these traditions, the two things that remain constant are the Wiccan Redes: Do What Thou Will As Long As It Harms None, and Whatever You Do Comes Back To You Three Times Three Times Three.

Faerie

Founded by Victor Anderson and Gydion Pendderwen, the Faerie tradition focuses on nature and ecological issues and concerns. Followers honor and revere the one creator and spirit and acknowledge this Divine light within every being. Followers also honor animal spirits and the power and protection they provide. They ascribe to the idea that life exists in a symbolic, transitory, and harmonizing spiral dance, nothing ever stays the same, and life is a swirling mass of constantly moving energy; this is similar to the Buddhist theory that there is impermanence of all mental states and material objects.

In the Faeirie tradition, emphasis is placed on Mother Earth's energy and her angelic protectors of nature, known as faeries. The word *faerie* is said to have its roots in the Gaelic word *sith* or *sidhe*, which has several meanings: hill or mound, Divine, unearthly, supernatural, and peace. *Faerie* is also said to have derived from *fatum* or *fate*, which means the Goddesses who control and rule over human fate; *fatare*, which means to enchant or mystify; and *fatuae*, which translates to a race of immortal feminine beings. Faeries are most powerful during the in-between times such as twilight and the moment just before waking up from sleep. The author Starhawk's books will provide you with additional information about the Faerie tradition.

Gardnerian

Gerald Gardner founded this sect of Wicca in England in the 1950s. He was the first to publicly speak about the Craft and we owe much of its survival to his courage. This tradition includes a degree system of advancement where no self-initiation is allowed. Covens perform magic in a circle of nine feet and skyclad (naked) in order to reduce self-consciousness or reservations that might obstruct the flow of magickal power.

They symbolically scourge themselves to purify and release unwanted energy. Some covens strive to have an equal number of females and males during ceremony; this is known as "perfect couple" and is a simulation of the perfect union of Goddess and God.

In their pursuit to attune themselves to nature, followers honor the God of the forest and the future as well as the Triple Goddess of fertility, creation, and rebirth. Followers emphasize the role of the Goddess over the God in ritual and worship. Many Wiccans debate about whether Gardner promoted an untainted version of an ancient religion, but it appears he was sincere in celebrating a happy, peaceful, nature-loving way of worship. The Farrars' books will be helpful if you are interested in this sect.

Dianic

Founded by Ann Forfreedom, this tradition focuses on feminist and humanist issues and concerns. Followers honor the Goddess Diana, encourage female leadership and matriarchal traditions, and celebrate mythos. Although members are primarily female, male participants are welcomed in some covens. There is a strong emphasis on the Goddess and her three aspects as Maiden, Mother, and Crone.

Followers live this tradition by ascribing to three basic values and ideas: self-awareness, kinship with nature, and sensitivity to the pulse and rhythm of the Universe. By accepting the human revolution around the axis that is the Goddess, followers strive to reawaken a heightened sense of compassion and understanding. Z. Budapest's books offer in-depth insight into this tradition.

Alexandrian

Founded by Alex Sanders, this tradition has rituals that are similar to those of the Gardnerian tradition. In contrast though, Alexandrians have a Judeo-Christian emphasis and embrace ceremonial magick elements. Ceremonial magick relates to the Judeo magickal system of corresponding the four directions into all aspects of the universe, which is also known as Kabbalah. Followers are traditionally more fixed in their beliefs.

Italian

Also known as Streghe, the Old Religion, La Vecchia Religion or simply La Vecchia—The Ways, this religion was taught by Aradia, daughter of Diana the queen of the witches, in the fourteenth century. Aradia taught The Ways by means of three traditions, known as the Fanarra—earth and forest mysteries, Janarra—moon mysteries, and Tanarra—star or stellar mysteries.

Followers believe in the Lare (also known as the clan spirits). The Lare are the most faithful people, and are believed to be born again and again to their descendants in order to remind us of all that is wise and sacred. Within their faith they also believe the one creator is both feminine and masculine, this soul/spirit lives in every being, and that reincarnation, karma, and psychic abilities all exist. Aradia also taught her disciples that we have power gifts, which include the ability to bring success in love; call forth spirits; hear the voice of spirit in nature; divine our future and hidden, secretive things; and bless, consecrate, and bring forth beauty. Read Raven Grimassi's books for more information about this tradition.

Norse

The Norse tradition is ancient and predates many of the other Wiccan paths. You do not have to be initiated to follow the Norse practice. Typically, rituals are performed clothed—often in traditional Norse garb. Followers honor and weave Norse mythology, ancient customs, languages, and pantheon into their magickal practice. They also place an emphasis on the sea. This has been attributed to the fact that the Vanir, an important Norse family of Gods and Goddesses, are believed to have descended from sea Gods and Goddesses. Norse followers also focus on Mother Earth; this focus is due to the Aesir, the Norse family of Gods and Goddesses, whose name translates to pillar or foundation.

The Runes, the ancient alphabet containing wise mysteries, plays an important role. According to mythology, the great Norse Father God Odin (also known as Wodin) willingly sacrificed himself to the world tree (known as Yggdrasil) by crucifixion in order to gain the Runic magick. Followers believe that this alphabet contain secrets of the universe, which are more important and essential than matter or energy. Freya

Aswynn's book, *Northern Mysteries and Magick: Runes, Gods, and Feminine Powers,* comes with a CD in which she powerfully chants the Rune alphabet in the ancient tongue.

Celtic

The Celtic tradition is also an ancient practice. It originated in the British Isles and has not been attributed to one teacher. This sect focuses on solar and lunar changes, the balance and harmony between the God and Goddess, and attunement with nature. Followers practice meditation, divination, and magickal herbalism. Emphasis is placed on the Celtic pantheon, history, traditions, food, and music. Solitary practitioners may find this tradition easy to follow since it does not require initiation.

Tree spirits known as dryads, the little people (also known as faeries), and water spirits, which are referred to as nymphs, all play an important role in the Celtic tradition. Read Edain McCoy's books for a Celtic version of Wicca.

Egyptian

The wise Egyptian teachings have existed for centuries. Followers of the Egyptian path stress the importance of magick, which they infuse in amulets, scripts, spells, names, and rituals. They believe in a central creator who exists in all beings. There is an Egyptian pantheon of Gods and Goddesses who host One Great Spirit. They believe that each human being is a compilation of nine separate bodies, and is blessed with resurrection, rebirth, and immortality.

The Egyptian tradition's foundation is a belief that the following sacred facts exist: divine truth, order and judgment, a divine battle between order and chaos, and a reverence and respect for all other paths. Eleanor L. Harris wrote an excellent book about Egyptian magick entitled, *Ancient Egyptian Divination and Magick.*

I suggest you research all avenues available to you before choosing your path. You should also familiarize yourself with the goddesses and gods throughout time and across the globe on pages 30–45. Modern Wicca is a culmination and gathering together of ancient wisdoms, incorporating these teachings into the needs and desires of today's busy world. Followers believe Spirit is constantly changing and being revealed to the blessed children of the Universe. We are each a ray of light from the great source of all that is. Therefore, any one of you can and will develop your own style of what Wicca means to you. There is no mediator between you and Spirit. You are the Goddess. You are the God.

MODERN WICCA

The word *witch* still scares many people; that's what genera-tions, and in fact centuries, of negative propaganda does. This bad press has brought on fear and a negative association with the term *witch. Witch,* as well as the word *Wicca,* comes from the Anglo-Saxon word *wicce* (pronounced wee-cha, with a soft cha), which means "wise" or "to bend or shape," particularly the shaping or bending of unseen forces. One example of this bending of unseen forces is the use of lemon to cut nausea. The nausea is the unseen force, and the lemony scent clears the mind and balances the body. Therefore, the one who prescribes the lemon is wise in that she or he is able to bend or shape the unseen force to her or his will. According to history, those who bent these forces were often designated the village midwife or herbalist. They understood which part of a plant, flower, or tree to use to heal a variety of illnesses.

Modern experienced witches are nonjudgmental, supportive, and accepting of all life paths. Witches do not fly around on brooms, hex people, practice infanticide, or consort with the devil (according to the Wiccan religion, there is no devil). The most important tenet of Wicca is this: Do what thou will as long as it harms none. Second, Wiccans or witches (many people consider these names interchangeable) abide by the Threefold Law: Whatever You Do Comes Back To You Three Times Three Times Three.

The Wiccan religion is a way of life and an approach to living. You can be a Catholic witch, a Jewish witch, Baptist, Hindu, and so on. Wiccans believe that we are a part of the harmony and rhythm of nature, that there is a necessary balance between dark and light, and that changing cycles of birth, death, and rebirth exist.

Quite often a person chooses the Wiccan path because he or she seeks more harmony within their self and their connection to nature. They have come to recognize they are merely an extension of the natural world, no more or less than the trees and stars. Wicca, like other earth- or nature-based religions, teaches that the same life force pulses through every rock, flower, person, animal, mountain, and body of water. Energy or light comes from the same source. You can call that source the Higher Self, Creator, God, Goddess, the Great Mystery, and many other names. This is the beauty of Wicca. As long as you harm none, followers accept all paths to Spirit. We are all here to teach, learn lessons, and experience life. How you walk your path is your choice.

No doubt about it, some people are interested in Wicca only because they want to learn spells and feel powerful. While Wicca makes you feel empowered, it also connects you to a protective, unconditional force that is larger and more powerful than yourself. If you pay attention to the spirituality and ideas on which the religion is based, you will gain an unshakable confidence and resourcefulness. You can choose to take a fish and let someone else feed you for one day (memorize one spell for one desire), or you can learn how to fish and feed yourself for a lifetime (understand how nature and spells work for the good and harmony of all and manifest your dreams).

This is a path that chooses you and that you choose. Just as some are drawn to the Greek pantheon, Christ's teachings, ancient paganism, or the wisdom of Buddha, some of you believe in all four as well as many other sources of wisdom. The reasons you choose to become, or actually awaken, the witch within are many: When you ask a question, you receive an answer; you feel you belong; it is a homecoming every day; you are at peace (or at least have crystal-clear moments of its serenity) with yourself and those around you; you feel a magnetic force drawing you to the Old Ways and/or nature; everything you ever learned during your lifetime begins to make sense; and other individual and personal reasons.

Why be a witch? You sense the connection between you and all that is. Wiccan teachings illustrate that you are the light. You have responsibility for your actions because Spirit wants you to be able to take full credit for your achievements—there are no failures, only lessons to learn and moments to experience. Spirit wants nothing more than the fulfillment of your every wish and to support your path to experience the joy, the stumbling and scraped knee, and the pride and confidence when you stand again. And you flourish, you blossom, you grow by leaps and bounds. You've come home.

TALKING ABOUT THE CRAFT

You might find that the more you get into Wicca and the Craft, the stronger the desire to share your experiences and understanding with others grows. Although sharing your practice with others can be exciting and fulfilling, it can also be devastating and result in a deterioration of your power.

Before you tell anyone, be it friends or relatives, you are interested or practicing the Craft, assess their ability to understand the religion and its philosophy. When I was first writing *The Wicca Cookbook: Recipes, Ritual, and Lore,* I took writing drafts to my writer's critique group. Without asking anyone what they thought about the subject, I passed out my samples. The next week, one of the girls looked at me with a horrified expression and said, "I can't review this for you." Another girl breathed a sigh of relief and said, "Yeah, it scared me just to read it." At first I was hurt and shocked. It took a while for me to get in the right frame of mind to pick up writing again.

But it taught me to consider my audience's ability to embrace certain levels of the topic. When I gave the book to a very Christian friend of mine, I used phrases and ideas we could both relate to, such as positive thinking, visualization, and "You reap what you sow," a version of the Threefold Law. After we came to an understanding of the similarities, she was able to overcome her anxieties and read the book, which she gave a rave review on the Internet. The important thing is to stay with the integrity of the Craft, but there is no need to scare anyone.

Choose your words carefully. Do not begin telling someone about Wicca using words like *cauldron, witch,* or even *spell.* There are a lot of misconceptions out there about Wicca. When you talk about the Craft to someone who is uninformed or nervous about it, proceed with caution. Your goal needs to be to educate them, not scare them. A frightened person is a dangerous person and one who may take action without thinking.

Another thing to remember is to keep it sacred. If you start blabbing about a spell you have cast before it has had a chance to materialize, it is as if you poked a hole in a balloon. The air or energy will leak out, and instead of being able to float out to the ethers and bring back your dreams, it will just weaken and fade away. In another analogy, it is like when you tell someone about a great dream. Of course you want to share it; it was so fabulous, and you believe that by sharing, you can make it more real. But what happens is the opposite. Each time you share the dream, you forget something about the sequence or the colors or what someone said. Instead of making it more tangible, it has begun to lose its essence and magick.

WICCAN HOLIDAYS

icca is an earth-based spirituality, which means followers live in tune with nature. Wiccans follow the cycles of the moon and the seasons and live in accordance with the natural rhythm of life. The Wiccan church is Mother Nature, whether we worship in a field, a forest, the mountains, the desert, or on a beach; and however you get there is just fine. Wiccans celebrate eight nature-based holidays (holy days) known as *sabbats*. Each sabbat connects us to Mother Nature with ritual and song that celebrates the ever-changing earth—so much like ourselves. These holidays, spaced six weeks apart, embrace special, sacred points on the Great Solar Wheel of the Year, also known as the Mandala of Nature.

Samhain
The first sabbat is Samhain, also known as Halloween, the third and final harvest or the witches' New Year, and is celebrated on October 31. During this holiday, decorate your altar with pomegranates, apples, pumpkins, gourds, pictures of deceased loved ones, autumn leaves, or marigold plants.

Samhain means "summer's end." It is the time of year that the veil between the two worlds is considered to be the thinnest, the world of the living and dead, human and faerie. Samhain is the time we trade information with people who have died and other spiritual beings as we give thanks for our loved ones. Death does not scare Wiccans because they recognize it as part of the natural cycle of birth, death, and rebirth. As the opposite side of death is birth, this holiday is the time for new beginnings and hopes for the manifestation of our dreams for the new year.

Winter Solstice

Winter Solstice or Yule follows Samhain, and it is the longest night of the year, falling between December 20 and 22. Possible altar decorations include evergreens, pinecones, wreaths, mistletoe, holly, candles, berries, or images of the sun. Some women stay up all night the night before the Winter Solstice to help Mother Earth get through the labor and birth of the sun. The darkness, the womb, is where all creation originates. It is a time of quiet reflection; if we pay attention to the voice inside, we can think clearly, and amazing ideas can be born. At Yule we celebrate the sun's growing strength. *Solstice* means "sun stand still," while *Yule* translates as "wheel." The wheel is symbolic of the Wheel of the Year, the ever-changing, never-ending cycle of birth, death, and rebirth.

Candlemas

Candlemas, Brigid, or Imbolc falls on February 1 or 2. Options for decorating your altar include candles, incense, seeds, nuts, vessels containing water, or herbal teas. This is the time of year when in the dark of a winter's night, the first seeds of light and inspiration are planted. We sow seeds and attempt to divine how long winter will last. This holiday is a perfect example of the Threefold Law: Whatever You Do Comes Back To You Three Times Three Times Three. You hold the paintbrushes to the canvas of your life. Whatever you sow, you reap; whatever you put out in the Universe comes back to you. Brigid, the goddess of fire, inspiration, and water wells, rules this holiday. She is the bride; her entire desire and purpose is to find her mate. Candlemas, along with the Roman holiday of Lupercalia that honors the god of nature and his passionate temperament, coincides with the modern holiday of St. Valentine's Day.

Spring Equinox

On the Spring Equinox or Ostara, which falls between March 20 and 22, night and day last equally as long. You can choose to decorate your altar with representations of spring and new life (such as rabbits, birds, baby animals, or flowers) or images of fertility (such as eggs, nuts, or seeds). Spring has begun, and with it, a celebration of rebirth and growth. Seeds planted in the darkness of winter are beginning to sprout and flower. Faeries, also known as nature sprites, are beginning to play again. The Spring Equinox is a time to honor the darkness and the light, to honor life and death, to explore the balance in our lives and nature, to give expression to our impish, playful behavior, and to cast spells for balance, harmony, and equality. This festival pays respect to Ostara, the German goddess of rebirth, dawn, and growth. All things green, fertility, and abundance are honored on this holiday.

Beltane

Beltane, also known as May Day, celebrates the pure joy of being alive and rejoices in all of nature's creations. Decorate your altar with flowers in a basket or alone, images of faeries, creamy treats for faeries, pictures of you truly enjoying yourself, maypoles, ribbons, or oak leaves and branches. It is the great spring festival of the Goddess. Gardens are beginning to grow, hibernating animals are waking, and all forms of creativity are celebrated. Beltane is also the holiday of fertility. On April 30 some celebrants light huge bonfires and literally party all night. The next day they erect a maypole (symbolic of the God) and wind ribbons (representative of the Goddess) around the pole. The result is the child. As fertility is a power-the power of creation—we must have respect for its strength and the results it brings. It must come at a time when we are mature enough to handle the outcome.

Summer Solstice

Summer Solstice, also known as Midsummer, is the best time to pick flowers for healing purposes. You can decorate your altar with flowers (especially roses), herbs, and pictures or other representations of the sun, such as a sunflower. Add anything to your altar that you are ready to give up. On June 20 through 22, the sun is at its strongest, and whichever day this holiday falls on will be the longest of the year. Since this is a fire festival, all things round, orange, or yellow are celebrated as a form of the life-giving sun, an aspect of the God. But as the sun reaches its full strength on the Summer Solstice, it, too, will begin to wane and fade in power. It is a reminder that life is not static; nothing lasts forever. Life, people, places, and things are always changing. Midsummer is the time to celebrate the joys life has brought you and practice letting go of things that no longer serve your highest good. This can be a painful relationship, old possessions, books, games, or a negative or destructive attitude. Cast spells for self-empowerment at this holiday.

Lammas

Lammas or Lugh is celebrated on August 1 or 2. Possible altar decorations include breads, corn, berries, grains, harvested fruits and vegetables, or pictures and symbols of all your hopes and fears for the coming year. The Wheel of the Year has turned to the first harvest. We reap the rewards of our hard work as we harvest corn and wheat. Because of the wheat harvest, this holiday is also known as the Festival of Breads. We are the guardians of all the seeds we have planted. On Lammas we begin the quiet season of facing our hopes and fears, as well as getting to know the unseen and hidden sides of ourselves.

Although the days are probably still warm, winter—also known as the "dark season"—is approaching, and so much can happen. It is time to make friends with our shadow selves, the part of our beings that points to where we need the most love and pure expression. It represents the areas that need either improvement or the light and space to shine.

Autumnal Equinox

The Autumnal or Fall Equinox, also known as Mabon, is the other day of the year (along with the Spring Equinox) when night and day are in balance. You can choose to decorate your altar with garlands of greenery and apples, harvested dried corn, winter squash, pomegranates, pumpkins, autumn leaves, nuts, or seeds. It is another season to cast spells for balance and harmony and to honor the cycle of birth, death, and rebirth as we begin the dark season of the Goddess. The warmth of the sun is fading, and the nights are getting longer. The Autumnal Equinox is the time for introspection and self-evaluation. This holiday marks the second harvest. As we gather the vegetables, fruit, nuts, and grain that are ripe, we give thanks. The Autumnal Equinox is the Wiccan Thanksgiving. We celebrate the coming of fall on September 20 through 22.

When you cast spells, try to match your focus with the nature of the season. Your spells will be stronger and work better if you do. Your spells need to be of a pure and good intent. It bears repeating that the number one principle of Wicca is:

Do What Thou Will As Long As You Harm None. That leads to the Wicca Rede: Whatever You Do Comes Back To You Three Times Three Times Three.

DEITIES AND SABBATS

Along with casting particular spells during certain seasons, your spells will also be more potent if you call on the guardianship, protection, and wisdom of that aspect of the Goddess or God that rules during that season. Wiccans honor the light in everyone as equal. We are all goddesses and gods, not just the prom queen or top athlete. When we cast spells and ask the protection or guidance of a particular deity, we call for that aspect of the Divine source to help our dreams come true. For example, if you wanted your crush to ask you to the dance, you might ask Aphrodite or Venus to help. If you needed protection, you could call on Hecate or Thor.

You will find that the deities who are associated with the same sabbats carry similar characteristics that are in harmony with the cycles of the season. For instance, during the Spring Equinox, many of the gods and goddesses are related to vegetation or fertility. The deities' attributes also pertain to the male or female contribution to that season. It will be helpful to incorporate this list of deities into your realm of magick.

SAMHAIN GODDESSES & ASSOCIATIONS

Al-Ilat *(Persian)* — moon magick, the Underworld

Baba Yaga *(Russian)* — the Crone

Bast *(Egyptian)* — cats, joy, music, dancing, healing, moon, fertility

Cerridwen *(Welsh-Scottish)* — wisdom, inspiration, new endeavors, shape-shifting, knowledge, magick

Epona/Rhiannon *(Celtic-Gaulish)* — mother, horse, abundance, change, moon, fertility, health, healing

Fortuna *(Greco-Roman)* — fate, luck (both good and bad), success

Frigg/Freya *(Norse)* — love, sexuality, war, protection, peace

Hecate *(Greek)* — moon magick, divination, the Underworld, justice, witches, dreams, knowledge, protection, success

Hel *(Norse)* — mystery, the Underworld

Inanna *(Sumerian)* — earth, love, weaving, battle, astrology, moon, rain, winged lions, prophecy, "Queen of Heaven"

Ishtar *(Babylonian)* — earth, fertility, love, battle, storm, marriage, divination

Kali *(Indian)* — destruction and death necessary for rebirth, justice, power, protection for women against violence

Lilith *(Hebraic)*	independence, obstacles
Mari *(Basque)*	moon magick, fire, earth, witches' protector, protection from lies, theft, pride, and arrogance
The Morrigan *(Celtic)*	water and its healing power, justice
Zorya Vechernaya *(Slavic)*	sun, Triple Goddess, well-being, protection

SAMHAIN GODS & ASSOCIATIONS

Am-Heh *(Egyptian)*	the Underworld, devourer, rebirth
Anubis *(Egyptian)*	death, health, wisdom, finding of lost things, protection, communication
Corn Father *(Native American)*	rebirth
Coyote Brother *(Native American)*	trickster, humor, nature
Ghede *(Vodun)*	death, resurrection, protector of children, healer
Hades *(Greek)*	the Underworld, elimination of fear
Loki *(Norse)*	trickster, cunning
Nefertum *(Egyptian)*	setting sun, lotus, shedding of old patterns or thoughts
Odin *(Norse)*	father, war, magick, poetry, cunning, the dead, creativity, divination

Pluto *(Greco-Roman)* — the Underworld, fortune, judgment, fire

Woden *(Teutonic)* — father, war, magick, poetry, cunning, the dead

WINTER SOLSTICE GODDESSES & ASSOCIATIONS

Changing Woman *(Apache)* — shape-shifting

Eve *(Hebraic)* — new life, creation, fertility

Gaia *(Greek)* — earth, love, fertility, heartbreak, marriage, divination, business

Heket *(Egyptian)* — childbirth, resurrection, frog

Kwan Yin *(Chinese)* — compassion, mercy, divination, magick, health, healing, protectress of mothers and sailors, depicted with a lotus

Lilith *(Hebraic)* — independence, obstacles

Ma'at *(Egyptian)* — justice, truth, law, Divine order of the universe, reincarnation

Metzli *(Aztec)* — moon and night goddess, agriculture

Nox *(Roman)* — night

Pandora *(Greek)* — truth, hope, gifts

Pax *(Roman)* — peace, harmony

Virgin Mary *(Christian)* — creation, purity

Yemana *(Yoruban)* — mothers, ocean, "Holy Queen Sea," the number *seven*

WINTER SOLSTICE GODS & ASSOCIATIONS

Aker *(Egyptian)* — earth, ability to see in both directions, the Underworld

Apollo *(Greco-Roman)* — sun, strength, courage, creativity, health, healing, justice, knowledge, intuition, success, heartbreak

Cronos *(Greek)* — doorways, possibilities, new endeavors, turn of the year

Father Sun *(Native American)* — sun

Helios *(Greek)* — sun, riches, enlightenment

Horus *(Egyptian)* — rebirth, sun, moon, prophecy, success, problem solving

Janus *(Roman)* — doorways, possibilities, January, new endeavors, turn of the year, overcoming of obstacles, opportunity

Jesus *(Christian)* — sun, rebirth

Llew/Lugh *(Welsh/Irish)* — sun, war, skill, art, smithcrafting, knowledge, "of the Long Arm" or "of Many Arts"

Oak/Holly King *(Anglo-Celtic)* — expansion and growth, restoration and withdrawal

Ra *(Egyptian)* — father, sun, light

Saturn *(Roman)* — faith, solitude, self-discipline, self-respect

Ukko *(Finnish-Slavic)* — sky, air, thunder

Yachimata-Hiko *(Japanese)* — possibilities, "innumerable roads"

CANDLEMAS GODDESSES & ASSOCIATIONS

Anu *(Irish)* — mother, abundance

Arachne *(Greek)* — spider, weaving, destiny

Aradia *(Tuscan)* — teacher, witch goddess

Arianrhod *(Welsh)* — mother, reincarnation, stellar movement

Athena *(Greek)* — wisdom, courage, war, protectress of architects, weavers, sculptors, smithcrafters, justice, creativity, business, depicted with owl, oak, and olive tree

Brigid *(Irish)* — fire, wells, inspiration, communication, poetry, creativity, smithcrafting, health, healing, new endeavors, opportunity

Februa *(Roman)* — cleansing, February

Gaia *(Greek)* — earth, love, fertility, business, heartbreak, marriage, divination

Inanna *(Sumerian)* — earth, love, weaving, battle, astrology, moon, rain, winged lions, prophecy, "Queen of the Heavens"

Pele *(Hawaiian)* — fire, volcanoes

Sarasvati *(Indian)* — creation, grace, science, teaching

Vesta *(Roman)* — fire, hearth, food, chastity

CANDLEMAS GODS & ASSOCIATIONS

Bannik *(Slavic)* — home, hearth

Braggi *(Norse)* — wisdom, poetry, creativity

Cupid/Eros *(Greco-Roman)* — love

Dainichi *(Japanese)* — purity, wisdom

Dumuzi *(Sumerian)* — vegetation

Esus *(Gaulish)* — vegetation

Faunus *(Roman)* — nature, dreams, prophecy, panpines, Lupercalia, vegetation, woods, cunning

Februus *(Roman)* — cleansing, February

Nurelli *(Aboriginal)* — creation, law, order

Prometheus *(Greek)* — intuition, wise advice, protection, fire, "He who foresees"

SPRING EQUINOX GODDESSES & ASSOCIATIONS

Aphrodite *(Greek)* — love, beauty, health, healing

Astarte *(Canaanite)* — fertility, love

Athena *(Greek)* — wisdom, courage, war, protectress of architects, weavers, sculptors, justice, smithcrafters, business, depicted with owl, oak, and olive tree, creativity

Coatlique *(Aztec)* — moon, earth, spring planting festivals

Demeter *(Greek)* — earth, abundance, fertility, barley, magick, wisdom

Eostre/Ostara *(Teutonic)* — maiden, beginnings, dawn, Easter

Gaia *(Greek)* — earth, fertility, love, business, divination, heartbreak, marriage

Hera/Juno *(Greco-Roman)* — home, hearth, moon, mother, protectress of women, marriage, peace, newborns, peacock for Juno, pomegranate for Hera

Iris *(Greek)* — communication, messenger of the gods, rainbow, new endeavors

Isis *(Egyptian)* — love, mother, beginnings, moon, disk and horns

Maia *(Greek)* — spring, rebirth, creativity, May, flowers, green, creation

The Muses *(Greek)* — inspiration, spring, memory, poetry, creativity, new endeavors, luck

Persephone *(Greco-Roman)* — the Underworld, rebirth, the dead, change, pomegranate, wisdom

Renpet *(Egyptian)* — seasons, spring, eternal youth

Venus *(Roman)* — spring, vegetation, love, ocean, "Star of the sea," mother, joy, "Queen of Pleasure"

SPRING EQUINOX GODS & ASSOCIATIONS

Adonis *(Greek)* — beauty, vegetation

Attis *(Persian)* — vegetation

Cernunnos *(Greco-Celtic)* — hunt, vegetation, magick

Dagda *(Irish)* — "Good God," magick, war, art, strength, music, wisdom, fertility, abundance

Dylan *(Welsh)* — sea

Great Horned God *(European)* — hunt, vegetation

Loki *(Norse)* — trickster, cunning

Mithras *(Greco-Persian)* — light, purity, victory, sun

Odin *(Norse)* — father, war, magick, poetry, the dead, cunning, creativity, divination

Osiris *(Egyptian)* — vegetation, fertility, reincarnation, crafts, justice, power, growth, stability

Pan *(Greek)* — vegetation, nature, woods, cunning, dreams, prophecy, panpines, Lupercalia

Xochipilli *(Aztec)* — "Flower Prince," corn, fertility, love, dancing, music, youth

BELTANE GODDESSES & ASSOCIATIONS

Aphrodite *(Greek)* — love, beauty, health, healing

Artemis *(Greek)* — ruler and source of water, moon, protectress of girls, good weather for travelers, courage, magick, healing

Cybele *(Greek)* — caverns, mountains, earth in its primitive state, crescent moon united with the sun

Diana *(English)* — hunt, athleticism, courage, wild beasts, moon, forest, abundance, heartbreak, liberation, success, wisdom

Erzulie *(Vodun)* — love, Triple Goddess, exuberance, generosity

Flora *(Roman)* — nature, flowers

Frigg/Freya *(Norse)* — love, sexuality, war, protection, peace

Gwenhwyfar *(Welsh)* — ocean, wisdom, balance, Triple Goddess, royalty

Ilamatecuhtli *(Aztec)* — "Old Princess," fertility, death, Milky Way

Ishtar *(Babylonian)* — earth, fertility, battle, storm, marriage, moon, divination

Maia *(Greek)* — spring, rebirth, creation, May, flowers, green, creativity

Prithbi *(Hindu)* — fertility, earth, grounding

Rainbow Snake *(Aboriginal)*   water necessary for life, menses, justice, magick

Shiela-na-gig *(Irish)*   great mother in primitive form, protection

Xochiquetzal *(Aztec)*   "flowers abound," all possibilities, beauty, joy, moon, love, marriage, art, singing, dancing, spinning, weaving, marigolds

BELTANE GODS & ASSOCIATIONS

Arthur, King *(Welsh-Cornish)*	hunt
Baal *(Phoenician)*	fertility, vegetation, storms
Cernunnos/Herne *(Greco-Celtic)*	hunt, vegetation, magic
Cupid/Eros *(Greco-Roman)*	love
Faunus *(Roman)*	vegetation, nature, woods, cunning, dreams, prophecy, panpines, Lupercalia
Frey *(Norse)*	fertility
Great Horned God *(European)*	hunt, vegetation
Lono *(Polynesian)*	fertility
Manawyddan *(Welsh)*	sea
Odin *(Norse)*	father, war, magick, poetry, the dead, cunning, creativity, divination
Pan *(Greek)*	vegetation, nature, woods, cunning, dreams, prophecy, panpines, Lupercalia

| **Puck** *(English)* | cunning |
| **Telipinu** *(Hittite)* | fertility |

SUMMER SOLSTICE GODDESSES & ASSOCIATIONS

Aestas *(Roman)*	Midsummer
Aine *(Irish)*	moon, meadows, Midsummer
Artemis *(Greek)*	ruler and source of water, moon, protectress of girls, good weather for travelers, courage, magick, healing
Athena *(Greek)*	wisdom, courage, war, protectress of architects, weavers, sculptors, smithcrafters, business, justice, depicted with owl, oak, and olive tree
Eos/Aurora *(Greek)*	day, youth, beauty
Erce *(English)*	fruitful womb, early name for Mother Earth
Gokarmo *(Tibetan)*	"She of the White Raiment," mother
Hathor/Tiamet *(Egyptian)*	pleasure, joy, love, music, dancing, beauty, responsibility, friendship, creativity, moon, marriage, art, prosperity
Hera/Juno *(Greco-Roman)*	home, hearth, moon, mother, protectress of women, marriage, peace, newborns, peacock for Juno, pomegranate for Hera

Isis *(Egyptian)*	love, mother, beginnings, moon, disk and horns
Kali *(Hindu)*	destruction and death necessary for rebirth, justice, power, protection for women against violence
Marici *(Tibetan)*	power, day's first ray of light
Nut *(Egyptian)*	sky, stars, early morning, womb, dead
Sekhmet *(Egyptian)*	war, sun, divine order, fierceness, power
Zoe *(Greek)*	life force

SUMMER SOLSTICE GODS & ASSOCIATIONS

Apollo *(Greco-Roman)*	sun, strength, courage, creativity, health, healing, heartbreak, justice, knowledge, intuition, success
Baal *(Phoenician)*	fertility, vegetation, storms
Dagda *(Irish)*	"Good God," magick, war, art, strength, music, wisdom, fertility, abundance
El *(Hebraic)*	father, life cycles, fertility, water
Gwydion *(Welsh)*	music, reincarnation, vegetation
Helios *(Greek)*	sun, riches, enlightenment
Jupiter *(Roman)*	faith, vitality, joy of living, business, confidence, prosperity
Mars *(Roman)*	war, courage, strength

Maui *(Polynesian)*	sun, fishing, fire
Oak/Holly King *(Anglo-Celtic)*	expansion and growth, withdrawal and rest
Ra *(Egyptian)*	life-giving sun, wealth, power, fertility
Sol *(Greco-Roman)*	sun, "Unconquered"
Thor *(Norse)*	sky, thunder, hammer, working class, justice, legalities, Thursday, strength, marriage, protection
Xiuhtecutli *(Aztec)*	fire, sun, "Lord of the Year"
Zeus *(Greco-Roman)*	father, power, protection

LAMMAS GODDESSES & ASSOCIATIONS

Cabria *(Phoenician)*	primordial mother, mystery
Ceres *(Roman)*	corn
Chicomecoatl *(Aztec)*	maize, goddess of rural plenty
Frigg/Freya *(Norse)*	love, sexuality, war, protection, peace
Habondia *(German-Celtic)*	witch, abundance
Hani-Yasu-NoKami *(Japanese)*	earth, substance
Ishtar *(Babylonian)*	earth, fertility, love, battle, storm, marriage, divination
Libera *(Roman)*	wine, fertility
Mama Alpa *(Incan)*	earth, harvest, abundance
Nisaba *(Chaldaean)*	grain harvest

Saning Sri (Japanese) rice, harvest, abundance

Tea/Tara *(Irish/Hindu)* star, education, ocean, sun, wishes, happiness, harmony, healer of sorrows, protection from fears and suffering

Tuaret *(Egyptian)* protectress of pregnant women

LAMMAS GODS & ASSOCIATIONS

Athtar *(Phoenician)* sun

Bes *(Egyptian)* merrymaking, music, protector of families, marriage, and children

Bran *(Welsh)* war, blessings

Dagon *(Phoenician)* agriculture, especially corn

Ebisu *(Japanese)* labor, fish

Ghanan *(Mayan)* agriculture

Liber *(Roman)* virility, fertility, vineyards

Llew/Lugh *(Welsh/Irish)* sun, war, skill, art, smithcrafting, knowledge, "of the Long arm" or "of Many Arts"

Odin *(Norse)* father, war, magick, poetry, the dead, cunning, creativity, divination

Xochipilli *(Aztec)* "Flower Prince," corn, fertility, love, dancing, music, youth

AUTUMNAL EQUINOX GODDESSES & ASSOCIATIONS

Akibimi *(Japanese)* — autumn

Chang O *(Chinese)* — moon, reincarnation, new moon

Demeter *(Greek)* — earth, abundance, fertility, barley, magick, wisdom

Epona/Rhiannon *(Celtic-Gaulish)* — mother, horse, abundance, change, moon, fertility, health, healing

Harmonia *(Greek)* — harmony

Lakshmi *(India)* — good fortune, prosperity, beauty

Modron *(Welsh)* — earth, abundance, fertility, barley

Morgan *(Welsh-Cornish)* — water, magick

The Muses *(Greek)* — inspiration, memory, poetry, luck, spring, creativity, new endeavors

Nikkal *(Canaanite)* — abundance

Pamona *(Roman)* — dove, peace

Persephone *(Greco-Roman)* — the Underworld, rebirth, the dead, change, pomegranate, wisdom

Rennutet *(Egyptian)* — nourishment

Snake Woman *(Native American)* — transformation

Sophia *(Greco-Hebraic)* — holy wisdom found within

AUTUMNAL EQUINOX GODS & ASSOCIATIONS

Bacchus/Dionysus *(Greco-Roman)*	vegetation, fertility, revelry, wine, reincarnation
Great Horned God *(European)*	hunt, vegetation
Haurun *(Canaanite)*	healing, death and rebirth, protection from wild animals
Hermes *(Greek)*	messenger of the gods, communication, trickster, commerce, travel, knowledge
Hotei *(Japanese)*	laughter, happiness
Mabon *(Welsh)*	hunter, fertility, reincarnation
Orcus *(Roman)*	death, the Underworld
Thoth *(Egyptian)*	wisdom, writing, communication, divination, magick, inventions, commerce, healing, initiation, success, truth

TOOLS OF THE CRAFT

his is the fun part: the tools, gadgets, and instruments of power. Most Wiccans have tools that help them with their magick. It is important to remember that while tools enhance spells and help you focus, it is your individual personality and intent that is the driving force behind each magickal incantation.

Some tools you may want to include in your witchy bag include an *athame* (ritual knife used for ceremony), bells, a Book of Shadows (secret diary of spells, rituals, or dreams), a *boline* (knife for cutting herbs), a *besom* (broom), a *burin* (engraving tool), candles, cauldrons, chalice, crystals, drums, gems, incense, jewelry, pentacles, rattles, rune stones, statues, swords, tarot cards, and wands.

You can get many of these items in metaphysical or other earth-based spirituality stores, even in health-food markets (check the Resource Guide on page 263). Tools are drawn to you, sometimes as a gift or other exchange. When you buy your tools, never haggle or attempt to bargain over the price, as it is considered bad form and will diminish the tool's power.

Often your tools can be made from items found in nature. Brooms are made from rowan, oak, ash, or birch trees, while wands come from hazel, oak, or apple branches. Although these are the most common tree branches and considered the most powerful, you can make a broom out of whatever is available or sacred to you. If possible, pick branches that have fallen on the ground. If none have fallen but some are hanging, ask for permission and direction on which branch to take. You will find your hand will be guided to the branch, flower, or whatever part of the plant or tree that nature wants you to have. When you take from nature, it is wise to ask permission and always give thanks.

To make the tools specifically yours, you must cleanse them of past energies and fill them with your unmatched power. To charge your tools, perform the following consecration ritual on the night of a full moon.

Mix spring water with sea salt in a chalice or cauldron. Sprinkle the salted water over your tools and say

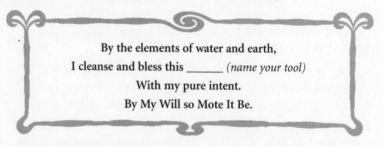

By the elements of water and earth,
I cleanse and bless this _____ (name your tool)
With my pure intent.
By My Will so Mote It Be.

Light a stick of incense, preferably cinnamon, eucalyptus, honeysuckle, or frankincense. Wave the perfumed smoke over

THE TEEN SPELL BOOK

your tool and say

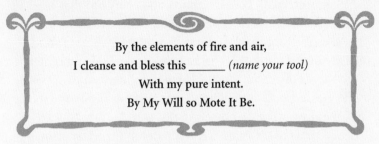

By the elements of fire and air,
I cleanse and bless this _____ *(name your tool)*
With my pure intent.
By My Will so Mote It Be.

Place your tools in the light of the full moon, and leave them overnight. You can leave the tools either outside or inside, although leaving them outside is more powerful. Use your tools regularly, and soon they will be charged with your individual power. You may also want to create an altar for your tools. An altar can be a dresser, nightstand, television tray, table, windowsill, shoe box, or anything that works and feels right.

CHAKRAS

The tools you bless will have an extraordinary amount of power, but there are also other tools, tools that have more strength than anything found in nature. These resources, known as chakras or energy centers, are found in your own body. Each chakra has a specific function or job, resonates to an element of nature or Spirit, and has a corresponding color. Chakras are like currents or vortexes, each representing a multitude of emotions, concerns, or obstacles that intersect at that chakra's function. Meditations and visualizations often use the chakras to bring power, balance, and energy to that area.

The first chakra is red, resonates to the earth element, and is known as the root chakra, or in Sanskrit, *muladhara*. Found at the base of the spine, this chakra helps us ground and center. It is the source of action, vitality, balance, solidarity, our survival mode, possessions, our ability to manifest our needs and focus, and rules over what we possess in this world.

The second chakra is orange, resonates to the water element, controls our sexual energy and intuition, and is known as the seat of life or in Sanskrit is known as *svadhisthana*. This chakra is located about two inches below the belly button. It is the center of fluidity, change, motion, nurturance, sexuality, and pleasure. It is the place where our duality of our feminine and masculine energies unite.

The third chakra is yellow, resonates to the fire element, and is known as the solar plexus, or in Sanskrit as *manipura*. This chakra, located between the navel and diaphragm, is the center of will, laughter, joy, anger, passion, transformation, power, fortitude, and energy.

The fourth chakra is green, resonates to the air element, and is known as the heart center, or in Sanskrit as *anahata*. Located at the heart, it is associated with pink since it corresponds to rose quartz, which empowers unconditional love. This is where we connect to relationships, gentleness, innocence, acceptance, balance, loss of ego, *prana* (the breath of life), and the Mother of all.

The fifth chakra is blue, resonates to sound, is located in the throat, and is known as the throat chakra, or in Sanskrit as *visuddha*. It controls creativity, order, language, eloquence, and the transformation of thought into words—also known as verbal communication. Often people will have a sore throat over and over again when they feel stifled and unable to communicate their feelings into words.

The sixth chakra is purple, resonates to light, and is known as the third eye, or in Sanskrit as *ajna*. This light center, located slightly above the space between the eyebrows, guides our inner sight. It is the center of perception, imagination, intuition, awareness, healing, and nonverbal communication.

The seventh chakra is white, resonates to thought, and is known as the crown chakra, or in Sanskrit as *sahasrara*. This chakra, located on top of the head, connects us with Spirit and works as a passageway for Divine understanding and knowledge, cosmic consciousness, connectedness, organization, and information. Christianity adopted this chakra when they placed halos atop their saints, angels, and the holy family.

ANIMAL TOTEMS

Another inner instrument of power lies in your connection to animals. Each of the animals listed below offers a gift or source of power for you. When you find which animal calls to you, you will find a friend, a comrade in good times and bad. If you are not sure who your power animal is, turn to page 126 for the spell and ritual.

Bat	brings rebirth, power to overcome obstacles, knowledge of past lives, inner strength, fortune, and happiness.
Bear	brings insight, introspection, inner knowledge, healing, prophetic dreams, and increased intuition.
Beaver	brings resourcefulness, security, achievement, hard work, and is a builder.
Buffalo	brings prayer, abundance, strength, potency, and alertness.
Butterfly	brings self-transformation, beauty, harmony, ever-changing cycles of life, and joy.
Cat	brings self-assuredness, independence, healing, love, and a sign that you can and will land on your feet.
Coyote	brings cunningness, trickster, medicine, humor, shape-shifting, and opportunity.
Crow	brings justice, Divine order, law, shape-shifting, cunning, boldness, and prophecy.
Deer	brings spiritual knowledge, patience, unconditional love, gentle courage, dreams, psychic power, graceful strength, and leads us to Faeryland or other worlds.

Dog   brings loyalty, love, camaraderie, devotion, alertness, truth, and is territorial.

Dolphin   brings playfulness, manna (breath of life), intelligence, deep wisdom, friendship, trustworthiness, eloquence, balance, and harmony.

Dragonfly   brings illusion, magic, dreams, wisdom, enlightenment, and truthfulness.

Eagle   brings spiritual transformation, wisdom, keen sight, connection to divinity, and courage.

Elk or **Stag** brings stamina, passion, endurance, patience, and camaraderie.

Fox   brings camouflage, cunning, intelligence, shape-shifting, and wisdom.

Frog   brings cleansing, transformation, fertility, and release from holding on to emotions.

Hawk   brings communication, magic, observation, transformation, strength, and is a messenger of the gods.

Horse   brings power, freedom, stamina, friendship, journeys, and faithfulness.

Hummingbird brings joy, love, possibilities, and happiness.

Lizard   brings dreams, stillness, guidance, and clarity.

Moose   brings self-esteem, wisdom, stability, and accomplishment.

Mountain Lion brings leadership, fierceness, power, and grace.

Mouse   brings scrutiny, inconspicuousness, and is detail oriented.

Opossum   brings diversion, strategy, and cleverness.

Otter   brings female creative energy, magic, joy, friendship, playfulness, generosity, and curiosity.

Owl	brings wisdom, deception, dreams, shape-shifting, keen insight, clairvoyance, and magick.
Porcupine	brings innocence, humility, playfulness, trust, faith, and gentleness.
Rabbit	brings hidden teachings, quickness of thought and action, and tends to bring our worst fears toward the forefront while giving us quiet strength and comfort to conquer this false evidence appearing real.
Raven	brings magic, shape-shifting, spiritual messages, eloquence, and prophecy.
Salmon	brings wisdom, inner knowledge, faith, fertility, journeys, magick, and endurance.
Skunk	brings respect, charisma, and integrity.
Snake	brings sensuality, change, creation, enables you to release old habits, and represents the seven chakras or energy centers within your being.
Spider	brings weaving, harmony, infinite possibilities, beginnings, and fate.
Squirrel	brings abundance, thoughtfulness, gathering, harmony, patience, endurance, and balance of work and play.
Swan	brings grace, power, femininity, dreams, dignity, intuition, and knowledge.
Turtle	brings fertility (as it represents the womb of the Mother), Goddess energy, creativity, patience, and perseverance.
Weasel	brings stealth, foresight, ingenuity, energy, and adaptability.
Whale	brings record keeping (the history of Mother Earth), balance, music, vastness, family, polarity, and clairvoyance.

THE TEEN SPELL BOOK

Wild Boar   brings confrontation, resolution, power, cunning, intelligence, defense, magick, prosperity, death, and rebirth.

Wolf   brings protection, knowledge, cunning, intelligence, independence, is a teacher, territorial, and represents the pathfinder.

RUNES

The Runic alphabet has been used for centuries to symbolize cosmic energies and for divination. This chart outlines the basic meanings and uses of the runes. Using runes themselves or drawing or inscribing the symbols on paper or other objects and keeping them on your person or in your home can help to magnetize appropriate energies to achieve goals.

Fehu

Money, property, power. This rune stands for creative power, fertility, and prosperity. Good for helping develop psychic abilities, to increase wealth, self-promotion, and harnessing the energy of cosmic forces. Divination: Issues concerning money and material values are of concern. Can indicate gain.

Aurochs

This is the rune of physical strength, vitality, wisdom, and healing. Brings understanding of the self. Helps imagination and visualization. Divination: Indicates a strong position. Strength, endurance, and determination will assist you in present situations.

Thurisaz

The rune of self-defense, applied power, and rebuilding after crisis. Helps ward off negative influences and awakens willpower. Good for

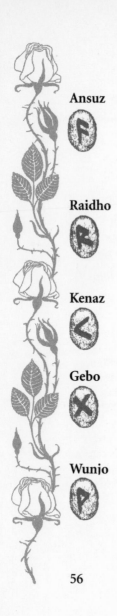

increasing assertiveness. Divination: A problem or crisis is beginning to surface and you must take action to protect yourself and change the energy.

Ansuz

The rune of communication with spirit, ecstasy, and inspiration. Aids communication with others, enhances psychic awareness, visualization, and self-hypnosis. Promotes fearlessness and understanding of death mysteries. Divination: Important messages are coming from others and from Spirit. Open to receive them.

Raidho

The chariot rune assists those on a journey, both spiritual or literal. The symbol for justice, ceremony, and magick. Awakens the inner voice and tunes us to earth rhythms. Assists travelers. Divination: You are undertaking a journey, trip, or vision quest that will have powerful results.

Kenaz

The fire rune stands for creativity, sexual energy, and transformation. Brings strength, healing, and awakens passion. Opens the door to sexual intimacy and artistic inspiration. Divination: A doorway is opening to a new and inspiring cycle.

Gebo

The rune of partnership, sex, and giving. This rune aids in achieving harmony in any kind of relationship, particularly intimate ones. Brings unity and connection with others. Divination: Achieving balance in relationships is important at this time. Love unconditionally.

Wunjo

The rune of joy and well-being. Strengthens bonds between people. Banishes feelings of alienation. Divination: Positive, optimistic vibrations are beginning to affect you and motivate your life. Peace and happiness can be yours.

56

Hagalaz

The rune of protection and banishment. Use to dispel negative influences. Helps us to evolve and move through difficult times. Brings balance. Divination: Difficulties help bring awareness of inner strength and truth. Be calm and centered and control negative thoughts and influences.

Naudhiz

The rune of deliverance from need or stress. Helps us recognize needs and find ways to meet them. Dispels hate and anger. Opens us to spirit help. To attract a lover. Divination: Use your limitations as a strength instead of weakness. Times of restraint require extra faith and focus.

Isa

The ice rune stands for the ego and controlling the will. Helps concentration and controlling unwanted influences. Divination: This may be a time of standing alone. Do not let fear rule you. Concentrate and center yourself and you will achieve clarity.

Jera

The harvest rune represents rewards, manifestations, creativity, and fertility. Enhances work on long-term projects. Helps achieve peace, harmony, and enlightenment. Divination: Indicates success coming from your efforts.

Eihwaz

The rune of protection and endurance. Protects against hostile forces and people. Helps us to see the truth and talk to Spirit. Increases personal power. Helps remembrance of past lives. Divination: Stand up for your rights and call upon spirit helpers and guardians in times of need.

Perthro

The rune of fate helps us understand and recognize karmic lessons. Aids in divination and games of chance. Creates change. Divination: Soon fate will move and change will be revealed to you. Change will help you connect with your life path.

Algiz

The rune of magickal protection is associated with protection, defense, connection to God. Connects us to guardian spirits. Strengthens luck in all matters. Divination: You may be in a situation where you need protection and you will have it by connecting with inner strength and spirit helpers.

Sowilo

The sun rune connects us with our guides and helps attract positive, successful vibrations. Use this rune for winning and victory in all matters. Divination: Success, wholeness, and clarity enhance your life at this time.

Tiwaz

The warrior rune promotes justice, victory, and self-discipline. Helps us develop self-reliance, self-control, and sobriety. Helps in conquering fear and doubt. Divination: A fearless attitude is required now to advance toward your goals. Be strong. Powerful forces reside within you.

Berkano

The goddess rune rules birth, fertility, and motherhood. Helps bring in nurturing, positive, creative energy. Beautifies and regenerates. Aids in conception, pregnancy, and childbirth. Divination: The birth of a child or a new start in some life area is imminent.

Ehwaz

The horse rune symbolizes a vehicle to take us to other worlds. Enhances trust, loyalty, and marriage. Brings prophetic wisdom and swiftness to earthly affairs. Divination: Influences are coming that will get things moving in a new direction and motivate you. Can indicate an actual move.

Mannaz

Symbol for the self, this rune promotes intelligence, memory, and unlocks the "third eye." Good for test taking, studying, or interviews. Divination: Center yourself and think about your own goals first at this time. Self-knowledge, self-discipline, and self-love are the keys to your success.

58

Laguz

The water rune promotes growth, vitality, and flow. Opens up emotions and helps clear out negativity. Enhances psychic awareness. Divination: A flowing, receptive attitude will have a wonderful effect on your present situation. Pay attention to dreams and insights.

Ingwaz

The rune for gathering energy, meditation, and centering the self. Promotes fertility. Divination: Creativity flows from you and as you gather your energies and resources, you will find new avenues of self-expression.

Dagaz

The rune of illumination and breakthrough brings clarity and inspiration from within and above. Clears, balances, and brightens. Divination: You are about to make a breakthrough in some important area. Truth, light, and understanding are on the way.

Othala

Rune of the ancestors, brings sacred protection to the home. Helps increase wealth and property. Divination: The desire to stick with your clan and harmonize your home is strong. Sometimes withdrawal and healing are indicated.

The Blank Rune

This is the symbol of releasing control and allowing higher powers to guide you. Helps us foster faith and trust in the Universe and connection to our higher self. Divination: Transformation, change, the end of one set of circumstances and the beginning of another. Challenge that brings progress.

SPELL CASTING

hether you call it prayer, visualization, dreaming, or spell casting, the words we speak act as affirmation to the Universe. If you say you have a big nose, terrible acne, or are a flaky friend, you draw attention to that part of yourself. Everything you think or do *will* take form. You send a message, and Universal forces are set into motion as life reflects our words.

Spells and the tools of the craft are only as powerful as the emotions they raise inside you. If you believe the color yellow means "courage," then it will call forth that ability—to the extent you believe it represents that valiant aspect.

Spells are cast to enhance our lives and can clear the way for dreams to come true. It is a matter of changing your outlook. Spells are not cast on or over someone else and do not go against someone's will. You can try to help others along, but not forcefully. Even if a friend has bulimia or is painfully shy, if you tried to haul them out of the situation, they might lose the lesson being offered. Later they might walk into the same trap again, only ten times worse.

Spells are primarily used to discipline the mind to create the fulfillment of our wishes. Some Wiccans have come to the point in their practice at which they no longer need to cast spells to actualize or materialize their deepest desires. The magick they incorporate is merely a concentration of will and the art of getting results.

Once you truly understand you are one with nature and Spirit wants nothing more than your happiness and every desire met, you will begin to recognize the magick and see the energy flowing toward you. Because we are so powerful, we must be very careful before we direct our intent or focus on anything. You have heard the phrase, "Be careful what you wish for!" Before you cast a spell, remember the Threefold Law and ask yourself these four very important questions:

1. Is it necessary? Have you tried everything in the physical world to make this dream come true? In other words, if you want to be an actress, have you taken any acting classes, signed up for drama, or even studied movies or plays? You need to make the first attempt. Magick that is performed primarily for the sake of boosting your ego will have little power. Second, you have to ask for what you want. Yes, it is that simple. Sometimes our angels or guides are just waiting in the wings to be asked. Then you must sit still, be quiet, and meditate. Listen for the small still voice nudging you in one direction or another.

2. Is it what you really need? You may need a true friend, but you may be caught up in the belief that only the most popular girl or guy should be your best friend—otherwise,

your dream has not really come true. Imagine what your dream come true will feel like, not an exact shape or appearance of your wish. A true friend is loyal, compassionate, and available—anyone can be this, but if it is a particular image you want to have, that may not be for your highest good. Ending spells, prayers, or affirmations by saying, "This or better," is a great idea.

3. Will it harm anyone, including yourself? This follows the number one rule of Wicca: Harm to none. Sometimes it is necessary to experience hurt before a need can be met. It hurts to discover you are being shallow, but as you cast off unhelpful aspects of yourself, like a snake shedding its skin, your spells will manifest more smoothly and more quickly.

4. Are you willing to own the responsibilities of the results? Once you have asked the forces of the Universe to shake, rattle, and roll so you can achieve your wish, you must accept the form Spirit has decided will best fit your need. It is like shaking a tree to get the leaves to fall; you cannot determine where they land, only the intent and energy you put behind your action. Remember, in Spirit anything is possible, including those things we cannot conceive.

The art of transforming a spiritual or mental idea into the physical world is awesome, quite empowering, and is one of life's greatest joys. As your intuition grows, you will come to recognize life's smallest gifts manifesting every day. You will clear the way for desires to come through you smoothly and effortlessly. Good luck, and may the Goddess and God light your path with love and light.

CASTING A CIRCLE

Casting a circle is an important first step for spellwork. When you cast a circle, you literally set down or place a magickal ring on the ground. As you cast spells within this sacred ground, you create a doorway for powerful, mystical events to take place. Setting a circle usually consists of the following guidelines, but how you choose specifically to create a circle is up to you.

1. Purify, cleanse, and protect each member participating.
2. Ask for protection from the four directions and your guides, angels, or companions.
3. Give an offering to the God and Goddess.
4. Set up the cone of power.
5. Ask for your desire to be met.
6. Give thanks to the directions, your guides, and the God and Goddess for being with you.
7. Lastly close the circle.

On your path through Wicca or any spirituality, you will encounter many different ways of practicing magick. All ways are okay as long as they harm none. Here is an example of circle casting:

Purify, Cleanse, and Protect Each Member Participating

Light dried sage leaves and let them ember (like a punk on July 4 or a stick of incense). Use an abalone shell or another fire-retardant container to catch the ashes. Direct the smoke toward you in a sweeping motion with a feather (a turkey feather works best; you can even tie beads or special gems to the end of the feather). Waft the smoke all around you, and visualize all bad energy leaving your aura and immediate surroundings while clearing the way for good vibrations. Be sure to visually send positive energy to your heart center. In other words, without touching your heart, try to imagine sensation in the middle of your chest. This is where your spells will originate. Pass the sage in a clockwise (deosil) direction to the next participant. If you are by yourself, just set the vessel in the center of your circle or altar.

Ask for Protection from the Four Directions and Your Guides, Angels, or Companions

After everyone is cleansed, hold the smoldering sage in the direction of east. Ring bells and say

Welcome, guardians of the Eastern Quadrant: Element of Air.
Bring us your gifts of inspiration, mental clarity, and new beginnings.
We do stir, summon up, and call you forth to this ceremony
That you may grant us your protection and wisdom.

Move to the south, ring bells, and say

Welcome, guardians of the Southern Quadrant: Element of Fire.
Bring us your gifts of will, courage, and action.
We do stir, summon up, and call you forth to this ceremony
That you may grant us your protection and wisdom.

Move to the west, ring bells, and say

Welcome, guardians of the Western Quadrant: Element of Water.
Bring us your gifts of emotions, serenity, and compassion.
We do stir, summon up, and call you forth to this ceremony
That you may grant us your protection and wisdom.

Move to the north, ring bells, and say

Welcome, guardians of the Northern Quadrant: Element of Earth.
Bring us your gifts of stability, instinct, and confidence.
We do stir, summon up, and call you forth to this ceremony
That you may grant us your protection and wisdom.

Give an Offering to the God and Goddess

Suitable offerings for the aspect of Divinity that we call the God include breads, corn, or wheat. Take the offering for the God, for instance, cornmeal, and sprinkle it as you walk in a clockwise direction. Alternatively, you can pass bread around the circle for everyone to eat. Be sure to leave a piece for the God in the center of your circle or altar. As the offering goes around the circle, say

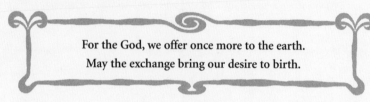

For the God, we offer once more to the earth.
May the exchange bring our desire to birth.

The Goddess prefers liquids, especially apple or passion fruit juice, which is just like her flowing self. Trickle the offering for the Goddess on the ground as you walk in a clockwise direction. As you distribute the offering, say

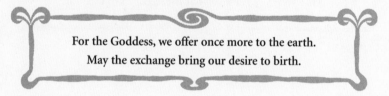

For the Goddess, we offer once more to the earth.
May the exchange bring our desire to birth.

Set Up the Cone of Power

Imagine the energy you have created encircling your group three times. Visualize in your mind's eye the energy spiraling up toward the moon. Your mind's eye is located between your eyebrows and is also known as the third eye or sixth chakra. As your web of energy and light draws nearer the moon, visualize this cone of power protecting you from negative influences while helping to direct positive energy from the Goddess and God to you.

Ask for Your Desire to Be Met

The time has come to cast your spell or make your wish. You may find yourself in a semitrance state; relax and let the rhythm flow, taking you where you need to go. It is like riding a canoe on a river or surfing a wave—when you try to fight forces greater than you, you invoke panic and lose the reason for your journey. You may not even realize you are in this dreamy state of mind until the circle is closed, so do not worry if you do not feel hazy.

Give Thanks to the Directions, Your Guides, and the God and Goddess for Being with You

After the spellwork is complete and/or you have asked for your desire, the time for gratitude has come. When you demonstrate your gratitude, you show proper respect for these great forces and deem yourself worthy of further help. The last two steps coincide.

Close the Circle

Always close the circle. This is a sacred space where you have drawn a metaphysical circle. It needs to be closed and safeguarded so all the spells you cast within will stay unbroken and beautiful. Hold hands with any members, and walk counterclockwise (widdershins) around your circle three times. On the first turn, verbally thank the four directions as you pass their stations. On the second turn, verbally thank your guardians and angels for their protection and guidance. On the third and final turn, say

O circle of power,
By our will, we release thee.
Thank you for your guidance.
Return to your place of power.
By Our Will so Mote It Be!

Clap hands loudly, or ring the bells again to disperse the energy. This action is like bursting a bubble or taking a broad expanse of energy and scattering it into a million parts to go out to the ethers and be transformed into your desire. With a broom or your hand, erase the doorway in the east. Lastly, erase the circumference of your circle.

Although it is not imperative to cast a full circle for every spell, it will focus your intent, and the sacred space will work as a magnet to draw in the elements and any assistance you need. You can choose to abbreviate this ritual for spells, or at the very least, you need to ground and protect yourself before all spellwork and magick is performed. One method of grounding and protecting begins with taking three deep breaths. Imagine a white golden light at your stomach (solar plexus), descending to the depths of Mother Earth. Once you feel centered, go ahead and start. You can cast a spell off-the-cuff with this quicker visualization and then repeat the spell under the protection and influence of a sacred circle.

THE FOUR DIRECTIONS

The pentagram, a five-pointed star, is a popular Wiccan symbol. The star is a representation of the four directions in balance with Spirit or love. If you combine the information here with pure intent, your spells will be more powerful, have more punch, and manifest more smoothly. For example, if you cast a spell for inspiration facing the east at dawn using a stick of incense or birds, your spell will have great strength. The combination of symbols that represent the same source will merge together like similar beams of light concentrated and empowered with your focus.

If a spell does not come to pass within three weeks, it is not that you did it wrong, it is just not going to happen. The Universe (or "one song": uni = one, verse = song) literally works in harmony for everyone on this planet. If your spell would harm someone, go against their will, had bad timing, or is just not meant to be, those Universal forces will scatter the energy before the spell hits the goal. And always, the Universe holds up a mirror to reflect back whatever you send out.

East

Element	air
Rules	inspiration, new beginnings, wind, mental clarity, psychic work
Time of Day	dawn
Season	spring
Season of life	childhood
Tools	thurible (incense burner), wand, bells
Sense	smell
Animals	birds, especially the eagle and hawk
Aspect of the Goddess	Maiden
Aspect of the God	Lad
Tarot suit	Wands

South

Element	fire
Rules	will, action, power, drive, life force, blood, healing, destruction
Time of day	noon
Season	summer
Season of life	puberty
Tools	athame, sword, thurible
Sense	sight
Animals	lion, horse, dragon
Aspect of the Goddess	Temptress, Enchantress
Aspect of the God	Adventurer, Warrior, Hunter
Tarot suit	Swords

West

Element	water
Rules	emotions, the womb, subconscious mind, love, adaptability, calmness
Time of day	twilight
Season	autumn
Season of life	maturity
Tools	chalice or cup
Sense	taste
Animals	water creatures and seabirds, especially dolphins and whales
Aspect of the Goddess	Mother
Aspect of the God	Father
Tarot suit	Cups

North

Element	earth
Rules	growth, nature, stability, money, silence, birth, death, sustenance
Time of day	midnight
Season	winter
Season of life	old age
Tools	salt, pentagram, boline
Sense	touch
Animals	stag, bison
Aspect of the Goddess	Crone, Elder
Aspect of the God	Sage, Elder
Tarot Suit	Pentacles

THE TEEN SPELL BOOK

THE MOON

Every culture and religion has its own language and symbols. There are limitless paths, but many people honor the influences of the moon. In the Spanish language, it is called *la luna;* in the Native American tongue, *miakoda* (power of the moon). The moon affects many things: It increases the size of waves, women's menses often begin with the full or new moon, and emotions run high during the full moon. Certain kinds of spells need to be cast at the different phases of the moon. In addition, for each month the full moon can enhance your spiritual and magickal work.

The moon represents the Threefold Law of Divinity as well. Known as the Triple Goddess, the moon reflects the Maiden in its growing crescent form and possibilities; it is the Mother when it is full and embodies fruition and attainment of goals and dreams; and last, when the moon decreases, it symbolizes the Crone in all her wisdom.

New or **Dark Moon**	This is the time to gain insight about oneself by making friends with our unseen or hidden aspects. We enter the stillness as we cast introspective spells. The moon is now hidden from view.
Waxing Moon	This is the time to begin new projects, plant the seeds of inspiration, and call on the Goddess as the Maiden. The moon appears as a crescent in a "C" shape.
Full Moon	This is the time to perform positive works, manifest spells that release your most passionate desires, and

focus on the Goddess as the Mother. The moon is now round and full.

Waning Moon This is the time for banishing spells, rituals for knowledge, and concentration on the Goddess as the Crone. The moon now looks like a crescent in a backwards "C" shape.

ASTROLOGICAL SIGNS

Astrology plays a major role with many Wiccans; of course, there are always exceptions. Planetary and stellar movements are popular and their courses are charted because Wicca follows the cycles and seasons of nature, of which the planets and stars are an integral part. The zodiac signs fall under the realm of astrology and are used to determine characteristics of humans, seasons, and phases of time that exist under their influences.

October—Libra *(Blood Moon)* Perform ceremonies for those who have crossed over to the other side, and give thanks for their gifts.

November—Scorpio *(Snow Moon)* Perform ceremonies for release from negative energy or bad habits.

December—Sagittarius *(Oak Moon)* Perform ceremonies for stability and conviction.

January—Capricorn *(Wolf Moon)* Perform ceremonies for security and comfort.

February—Aquarius *(Storm Moon)* Perform ceremonies for a bright future.

March—Pisces *(Chaste Moon)*   Perform ceremonies for right action and pure intent.

April—Aries *(Seed Moon)*   Perform ceremonies for the manifestation of the seeds of your desires.

May—Taurus *(Hare Moon)*   Perform ceremonies for abundance and new possibilities or beginnings.

June—Gemini *(Dyad Moon)*   Perform ceremonies for balance and harmony.

July—Cancer *(Mead Moon)*   Perform ceremonies for gratitude, and plan what you will do when your spells come true.

August—Leo *(Wort Moon)*   Perform ceremonies that incorporate herbs in spells, known as *wort cunning* (the magickal use of herbs).

September—Virgo
(Barley Moon)   Perform ceremonies for reaping the rewards of your efforts.

COLOR CHART

Colors are actually vibrating light. Depending on the frequency of this vibration, colors will affect our emotions at different levels, thereby they affect our spells. You can wear a certain color, burn candles of these hues, or just concentrate on light of a certain shade to help bring about your desires. The colors are listed in accord with the chakra system.

Red	passion, energy, will, vitality, power, strength, aggression, courage, life force, health, and achievement
Orange	spirituality, higher levels of awareness, attraction, mental energy, adaptability, motivation, harmony, encouragement, happiness, harmony, and the southern direction
Yellow	mental clarity, charm, friendship, communication, success, business, and the southern direction
Gold	solar energy, prosperity, confidence, and success
Green	money, calmness, nature, the northern direction, balance, job finding, luck, prosperity, fertility, love, and healing
Blue	truth, healing, decision making, tranquility, understanding, patience, self-awareness, health, dreams, removal of guilt, and the western direction
Purple	intuition, divinity, royalty, spiritual communication, ambition, and the eastern direction
Pink	unconditional love, romance, friendship, and protection
White	protection, blessings, purity, truth, healing, and meditation
Silver	meditation, negates stress, and hope
Brown	grounding, endurance, stability, home, security, and the northern direction
Black	unknown, removal of negativity, and banishing

DAYS OF THE WEEK

Each day of the week relates to different aspects of our lives and can infuse incantations with more power. There will come a time when you cannot cast a spell or ritual on the appropriate day, which is fine. Magick is practical and as long as your focus is pure and strong, your spells will reflect this. Whenever possible, though, correspond the intent of your spell or ritual with the natural powers inherent in the days of the week.

Sunday   is ruled by the sun and oversees friendships, jobs, the healing of Divine power, and intuition.

Monday   is ruled by the moon and oversees love, home, family, women, clairvoyance, subtle changes, medicine, the ocean, emotions, and dreams.

Tuesday   is ruled by Mars and oversees confrontation, battle, athleticism, hunting, surgery, physical strength, courage, contests, competition, and men.

Wednesday   is ruled by Mercury and oversees communication, computers, learning, divination, teaching, self-improvement, and intellect.

Thursday   is ruled by Jupiter and oversees wealth, legal matters, money, materialism, and luck.

Friday   is ruled by Venus and oversees love, music, pleasure, joy, and women.

Saturday   is ruled by Saturn and oversees terminations, the dead, reincarnation, elimination, faith, solitude, self-discipline, self-respect, and banishment.

SPELLS

pells open a doorway for our desires to come from the spiritual world and pass through into the material world and the earthly plane. Spells are taught as a teaching mechanism to help instruct people to focus their thoughts and intentions. Rhyming is used as a means of speaking to the right brain, the creative side. The rhythmic chant becomes trancelike, and we lose our logical side and begin to see the expression of our met desire, not the logical appearance of it. According to Scott Cunningham, a renowned Wiccan author of the book *Magical Herbalism* and teacher, "Ritual strengthens, defines, and directs magickal powers."

Spells and the tools of the trade are props, mnemonic devices used to represent a slew of information, a concept, or trigger a memory or dream. For example, an old baseball glove, trophy, or ribbon might represent a whole era of playfulness, while a pinecone or fishing hat can remind us of camping with Grandpa. A photograph can illicit the sounds and smells of the image captured, while a childhood teddy bear or other keepsake can symbolize a time of innocence and safety.

Some spells are very common; within the Craft we like to call them "cookbook" spells. You may have heard of or read some of these spells. They appear so often because they work and are simple, the reason being that the intent is the most important ingredient of all, not the symbols or tools. You may, of course, prefer more ritual than some of the spells offer, and I encourage you to add your individuality to the spells. Spells are like recipes and are almost always tinkered with to appeal to your unique appetite. Most of these spells will work over a period of time, while some will manifest within a day. Most spells will manifest in three weeks. If your spell has not materialized in six months, it is not going to happen.

You will get out of a spell exactly what you put into it, including your attention, time, effort, and energy. Focus your intent; an absent mind reduces the spell's effectiveness, while a concentrated mind boosts the spell's innate power. Speak your chants clearly and with conviction. Although it is okay to repeat the same spell for added power, casting more than three different spells a day will reduce their effectiveness. In addition, magick should not be performed for pay. The recipient may offer you another form of energy exchange, such as doing your chores or giving you a gift, and they always need to buy the necessary ingredients. At least one item in the spell has to have their energy.

Before you cast a spell, it is a good idea to test whether the spell is necessary and for the good of your spiritual and human being. Only you can determine this. You may want to try one of the following methods.

Take a pendulum (this can be a necklace, a chain with a crystal or other charm, or even a string with a needle attached to the end) and hold the lower end perfectly still. Ask Spirit whether or not you should cast the spell. Mention the type of spell and the desired outcome. Let go of the lower end of the pendulum. If it swings in a *linear* fashion, either back and forth or from side to side, the answer is no. If it swings in a *circular* motion, the answer is yes.

To get an even more accurate answer, hold the pendulum over a representation of the area that is bothering you. The following representations all correspond with the four directions, which you can look up on page 72 for more ideas. If you are having troubles with emotions, hold the pendulum over water or a chalice; if you are having troubles with grounding, hold the pendulum over a pentagram; if you are having troubles with clarity or intuition, hold the pendulum over a wand; if you are having troubles with action, hold the pendulum over an embering stick of incense.

You can ask the question by writing it with your dominant hand. Take three deep breaths, clear your mind of all thoughts, pick up the pen or pencil, and answer yourself with your weaker hand. This will transport you to the land of symbols and intuition.

Lastly, you may choose to mark stones with the words *no* and *yes*. Turn the stones over, and closing your eyes, mix them up. This will only work if you really lose track of which stone is which. Ask whether or not you should do the spell, and choose a stone.

EMOTIONAL, SPIRITUAL, AND PHYSICAL HEALTH SPELLS

BANISH SELF-DESTRUCTIVENESS

Self-destructive behavior can be defined as anything from cutting, drug abuse, giving away sexual power, bulimia, and anorexia to negative self-talk and all things in between. These patterns of behavior arise when a person feels out of control. Self-destructiveness provides a way to compartmentalize the unmanageable people and things in our lives and escape reality. But often the release becomes an addiction—compulsive and progressive.

This is a very important spell due to the intensity of it. I suggest you cast a full circle before casting the spell. Perform this ritual during the waning of the moon. Construct a white image candle. Inscribe your astrological sign and any personal symbols on it. Anoint it with oil of your zodiac sign. Surround the candle with three purple candles to represent clear vision. Anoint all the candles with Jupiter oil. Jupiter represents faith, the development of vitality, the joy of living, and confidence, and will help lift your state of mind. Imagine yourself as a diamond with many facets. These facets are the unique aspects of your personality, talents, emotions, and every part of yourself imaginable. It is your job to keep these facets or windows clean and clear. Divinity is a universal force from which light

THE TEEN SPELL BOOK

originates and radiates. When the facets of your diamond are translucent, Divinity/God/Goddess can shine through you. It is not your job to determine how good or valuable your assets are; your job is only to honor them, for they are gifts from Spirit.

It is not enlightening nor do you serve others when you make yourself small and pretend you are unworthy. You are many aspects of Divine specialness. Repeat this affirmation:

I am special.
It is safe to be me.

If possible and safe allow the candles to burn out themselves. Repeat the affirmation often throughout the following week. Allow yourself to be a channel for all the goodness inherent in your being and the Universe. Be gentle on yourself. There is only one you, and we need you.

(NeithSpell, a Wiccan High Priestess and owner of Points of Light, a store dedicated to providing everything metaphysical in nature [located in Long Beach, California], generously donated this spell and is an inspiration for others as well).

BE SEEN AS YOU TRULY ARE

Do you ever feel like absolutely no one understands you? Wouldn't it be nice if just one person could really see you? And not just know your favorite color, favorite food, or best dream date. Wouldn't it be nice if someone could see down to the core of your being, past all the walls and masks you put up, and see through to the little person inside, accepting you for all they see?

My grandparents do this for me. When I was on the edge of life, staring down into the abyss and just numb, they brought me back—not by force, guilt, shame, or any of those conventional methods, but just by being there. I got busted when I came in way past curfew; sometimes they looked away, but not before I caught the disappointment in their eyes. There was no drama, just a failure of my trusting them. Their belief that I would come back if they just mirrored stability worked. When I looked in their eyes and saw they believed I could refocus my life and begin anew, then I believed I could.

Look around. Is anyone trying to do this for you? You will experience many different things in life, and each will add a new dimension to your personality and frame of reference. Let's say you have nine facets (or sides), nine unique expressions of self. As you grow older and experience more, you will continue to cultivate those things that excite you and make you

THE TEEN SPELL BOOK

happy. This is especially true when we enter a new phase or level of life, such as school, puberty, adulthood, marriage, parenthood, or retirement. As we reveal new aspects of ourselves, inevitably we depart (sometimes momentarily), from others, even our closest friends and relatives. This is a very lonely state. When others only see two sides or parts of our selves, even if they truly love what they see, sometimes it just isn't enough.

First, this intent will change your life and most everything you know to be true. It is not a spell for everyone. With this incantation, you will become a beacon of light and love. It is the death of your old self and rebirth of a stronger you; an opening of your emotional and spiritual body, just as you would open your physical body, arms thrown open and chest exposed. As you become more open and accepting of yourself, you will radiate and draw others who are open to receive that light. We can see seven main colors with the naked eye, but so many more exist on the band of light. You are moving into the ultraviolet rays of being, and those who have crossed over will see you. When someone really sees to the depths of your soul, they reflect the light you reflect from Spirit; and through their eyes, you will see and love yourself beyond measure.

You will invoke Ganesha, the Hindu elephant-headed god of fortune, wisdom, and literature. Ganesha's main gift to humans is the ability to remove all obstacles. Place an image, whether it is a postcard, drawing, or statue of Ganesha, next to a white image candle (see page 260 for a description of an image candle).

Imagine white golden light swirling beneath your feet. Close your eyes and visualize this light entering your body through your toes and coursing through your body until it shines from the top of your head and through each finger. Watch as the white golden light moves to encircle you like a protective shield. Take three deep breaths. Inscribe the white candle with your astrological sign, magickal name, and/or favorite symbols. Anoint both the red and yellow candles with two drops of Ganesha oil to call in his assistance. Say

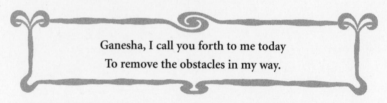

Ganesha, I call you forth to me today
To remove the obstacles in my way.

Rub sandalwood oil on the white candle, and imagine yourself infused with inner peace, balance, and relaxation. Add aura cleansing oil to clear away any mildew or dirt from your aura. An aura is like a bubble of energy that surrounds your entire body to about eighteen inches away from you. As you rub on this oil, see yourself as a clear quartz crystal. Imagine yourself wiping each facet clean, like you would a window.

When all your windows are clean, open your eyes. Thank Ganesha and douse the flame with a candle snuffer.

DEAL WITH ANGER

Anger is a result of not having our needs met. And let's face it, we all get angry over something on occasion, right?

Some people lose their tempers, with explosions of words and action. They explode because they know they can get away with it. Others express their anger in a quiet and sly manner, like a slithering snake; and when they strike, are venomous and cold.

It is *how* you deal with that anger that makes or breaks you. Staying in an angry mode and not processing it through is very dangerous for our bodies and minds. If you hold back your anger, then it builds to intensity until something else makes you snap! So bring it up and send it out.

Go outside and light a black candle. Focus on the flame; visualize it growing in intensity as you begin to think of something that made you angry. Take an egg and hold it lengthwise so your fingers are wrapped over the point. Grip the egg as tightly as you can, sending all your anger into it (if you hold the egg correctly, it will not break). Continue to let the emotion build as the flame becomes more intense. When you are really worked up about it, throw the egg as hard as you can, and yell, "*Be gone!*"

Take three deep calming breaths. Visualize the flame dying out as you gently form your hands around it. Say

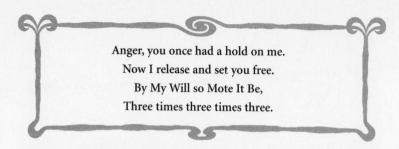

> Anger, you once had a hold on me.
> Now I release and set you free.
> By My Will so Mote It Be,
> Three times three times three.

Repeat it as many times as you need to. When you are ready, blow out the candle and say

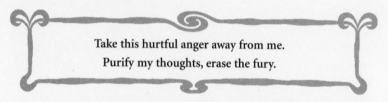

> Take this hurtful anger away from me.
> Purify my thoughts, erase the fury.

Visualize the remainder of your anger disappearing with the candle flame. Light a pink and a white candle. The pink candle represents self-love, and the white candle represents protection. Say

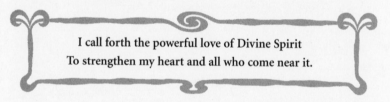

> I call forth the powerful love of Divine Spirit
> To strengthen my heart and all who come near it.

DEAL WITH CRITICISM

For some of us, criticism can be very difficult to deal with. First of all, you need to remember that the assessment received is only one person's opinion. We literally change who we are every day. New information, experiences, and even the food we eat plainly alter us. Take into account whether the criticism was constructive and meant as helpful or damaging and harmful. Realize it came from a unique, frozen moment in that person's life. You have no idea what happened to them moments before they criticized you. You received it at a unique, frozen moment in your life. The dynamics will never be repeated. Life is a dance, with the dancers constantly moving and shifting. Why should you hold on to something that may no longer be true, if it ever was in the first place?

Perform this ritual during a waning moon. Write down every nuance of the criticism on a piece of parchment paper. Highlight what is good or what can be construed as positive. Assess how you can improve the negative points. Write a new list, or make little posters, of what you can do well or affirmations of what you can do better. For example, if someone said you are selfish, write, "I am now free to give unconditionally." Tape these positive notes on a mirror, or put them in a desk where you will see them regularly. Take the first list and put it in the fireplace the next time your family has a fire, or burn it in a safe bowl. Say

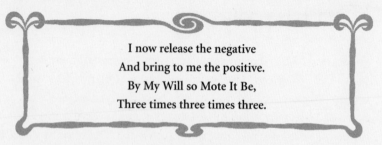

I now release the negative
And bring to me the positive.
By My Will so Mote It Be,
Three times three times three.

You can either bury the ashes or flush them down the toilet.

Deal with Teasing

"Sticks and stones may hurt my bones, but words will never hurt me" is one of the biggest fallacies children are taught. The concept is a needed survival mechanism, but one that has limitations and needs to be seen for what it is—a temporary fix. Words indeed hurt. Words are one of the most powerful tools and aspects of magick we have. With words, we command attention, divulge our feelings, and communicate our needs. Often teasing words seep into our skin and tear at our self-esteem. So do not think you need to abide by this saying any longer.

Regardless, if you cast a spell to make a bully go away, you still may have powerful emotions about being a victim. And this is where your true power lies. You have the ability to stop the pain. You can and will release their negative energy and rebuild your confidence, self-acceptance, or whatever else was damaged in the process.

Cast this spell on a Saturday. Anoint a blue agate, which is a stone that brings peace and alleviates depression, with one drop of honeysuckle oil, a scent used to bring joy. Light a white candle for protection, and anoint it with either Iris Goddess oil or iris oil from the flower. Iris brings wisdom, stress relief, messages to and from Spirit, and new endeavors. Rub the stone over your heart center, and quietly say

> Angels, spirit guides, guardians, and friends,
> Take away this pain that seems to have no end.
> Grant me the wisdom and strength to see my true light,
> I am lovable, worthy, and powered by a love so bright.

Take a piece of lavender cloth (for inner beauty), and place inside one bay leaf (to remove negative energy) and one teaspoon of cinnamon (for strength). Place the agate inside as well. Wrap the cloth and bind it with silver ribbon. Anoint it with sweet pea oil (or add the petals of sweet pea to the pouch). This flower calls forth the truth of any situation with its gentle power. Repeat the chant and visualize a hummingbird and its shimmering breast. A hummingbird embodies joy, possibilities, and happiness. Douse the flame with a candle snuffer. Repeat the chant every day for nine days, always envisioning the hummingbird. Also, do not be surprised to see the amazing birds appear.

THE TEEN SPELL BOOK

FIND PEACE AND SERENITY

Do you feel scattered? Do you have too many activities going on? Do you feel like the weight of the world is balancing on your tense and tired shoulders? Signs of an unbalanced life include a straight posture that grows limp, crashing as soon as your head hits the pillow or becoming an insomniac and walking zombie, being tired and lethargic most of the time, not being able to keep your attention on anything, and being, uh, crabby (that's the nice way to put it). Some days you feel like a newborn awakened by the USC marching band: There is way too much stimulation. Experts say in an urban environment we are bombarded with five hundred thousand sources of information and stimulation every day! When you add soccer practice, homework, flute practice, college prep classes, and karate, it gets to be a tad too much.

Conduct this spell for balance during a waning moon or at the Spring or Fall Equinox. Clear the clutter from at least one space, be it your desk, closet, or under your bed. Try to do this ritual in silence, or if you need some sound, listen to meditative music. Get rid of as much as you can—throw away trash and put the usable stuff in a donation box. Light a stick of sandalwood or nag champa incense.

Then lie down or sit. Close your eyes, and try to clear your mind of all thoughts. Hold down your right nostril for one intake of breath, releasing your breath from your left nostril. Then hold down your left nostril for one intake of breath, releasing your breath from your right nostril. Repeat this for at least ten breaths. Each time a new thought enters your awareness, turn it into a cloud on the screen of your mind and watch it leave. Try not to get attached to any one thought.

When you feel calm and centered, take an overall look at your schedule like an eagle purveying the forest for its next meal. View your to-do list as if it is not yours, from a distance. What is the first thing that looks out of place? What is the first thing that jumped out as not really serving your current needs? Hold your solar plexus, the center of courage and grounding, which is located between your ribs at your diaphragm. Breathe deeply three times and say

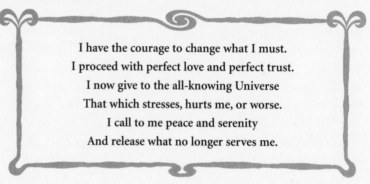

I have the courage to change what I must.
I proceed with perfect love and perfect trust.
I now give to the all-knowing Universe
That which stresses, hurts me, or worse.
I call to me peace and serenity
And release what no longer serves me.

THE TEEN SPELL BOOK

Repeat this chant every day for nine days. The repetition of the same prayer every day for nine days is called a *novena*. And most importantly, drop the first thing that popped up and clear your busy schedule. Approach each day with calmness, focusing on one event at a time.

FORGIVE SOMEONE

Forgiving someone does not mean you have excused or condoned her or his behavior. The reason to forgive someone is that resentment fosters anger, and anger corrodes the vessel that contains it. According to *Webster's New World Dictionary*, *forgive* means "to give up resentment against or the desire to punish; pardon; to overlook an offense; to cancel a debt." Thus, the goal of forgiveness is to let go of a hurt and move ahead with life.

Regardless of what they did to you, they did it to you once or maybe a few times. But every time you relive the incident, it is as if you do it to yourself again and again. Reliving painful events and situations brings toxins and other pollutants into your body. Your thoughts determine your health—both mental and physical. If you harbor and hold sadness in your heart long enough, it will eventually need to escape and find an outward expression, which can result in serious illnesses or, at the very least, restrained living.

Who has become the perpetrator now? You can forgive the offender and still choose not to reestablish the relationship. You shall not become a doormat or allow them to hurt you again.

A lack of forgiveness gives others power over you. Withholding forgiveness and nursing resentment simply allows another person to have control over your well-being. It is always a mistake to let such negative emotions influence your living. Forgive, and you will be able to direct your life with positive thoughts and actions.

To become a tolerant forgiver of major pains, first practice forgiveness on small hurts. Try this spell on small slights or insults, especially those inflicted by strangers—someone who cut in line, a rude salesperson, and so on. Use these events as practice to prepare you for the tougher task of forgiving major hurts.

During the waning of the moon, light a black candle for the banishment of your resentment. Burn frankincense and myrrh incense. Write a letter on a piece of parchment paper to the person who hurt you. Express fully, clearly, and honestly how you feel and why that person's action hurt you and made you angry. Say whatever you want, using whatever language fully expresses how you feel—you will not be mailing this letter, so you do not have to censor yourself either in anger or depth of sadness. Finish the letter with the bold declaration that you have forgiven him or her. Fold the letter and allow the wax from the candle to drip on the fold, sealing it. As you do this, say

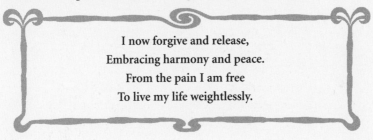

I now forgive and release,
Embracing harmony and peace.
From the pain I am free
To live my life weightlessly.

Then bury the letter somewhere in your yard or even in a distant field. There is no need to keep score of wrongs done to you. Spirit has built the real recorder into the system of the Universe. Known as karma, this system states that the one and only thing that can remove wrongs is amendment (correction or repair) of the wrong. Whoever hurt you will have to make a settlement. But that is a correction made to the Universe, not always to you personally. Recognize and reflect on this truth: Only people who are hurting lash out with anger, disrespect, or contempt. With this inherent pain, their payback has already begun. Do not attempt to bring on their retribution, or you will only accrue your own bad karma.

Forgive them, rise up in consciousness, become love; love is the master of karma, love forgives all.

Booker T. Washington (1856–1915) wrote, "I shall allow no man to belittle my soul by making me hate him."

FREE YOURSELF FROM DEPRESSION

Ancient Wiccans called depression by the names *melancholy* or *melilot*. Depression's dark energy get its vicelike grip on your heart and energy level. You become sad, lethargic, and defeated. The truth is you are still the light and love that originate from a source that encompasses a powerful and true love. You are not your depression: It is merely a phase, a feeling that has attached itself to you. Depression has an incredible ego that would have you believe you rarely existed without its dark, menacing cloak.

Cast this spell on a Saturday during the waning of the moon. Light a black candle. Pour clear, clean water into a glass, leaving about two inches at the top. Scoop up a fistful of mud. Focus your depression into the mud. It's murky, polluted, threatening, ominously gray, and foreboding. The mud will then represent all your fear, frustration, pain, hurt, loneliness, and so on. Plunk the muck into the clean water and say

> Depression, release your hold on me.
> Be gone! By My Will so Mote It Be.

Blow out the candle when you say, "Be gone!" Rinse your hands in a bowl of clean water with either lavender or rose petals floating in it. Over the next several days, you will begin to notice that the purity of the water, like the force of love, cuts through that mud and dissolves it. You must allow for some evaporation, adding water every three days. After two weeks, pour the water out in your yard or anywhere outdoors.

HEAL APATHY

Apathy is the terrible sensation of being in a black hole.
When you are apathetic, you don't care what happens today or
tomorrow; you are numb, feeling nothing but the impression
you are spiraling backward through a bleak darkness. It is not
always defined as boredom, lethargy, or laziness. You may be
fully functioning, but your indifference, lack of concern, and
inability to conjure an emotion of any reasonable size has
begun to really scare you.

I believe it is the gentle, fragile souls (like love or creation
itself), who feel deep pain and are ultrasensitive, who fall into
the trap of apathy. They have felt so much pain that they cannot
stand it, and they shut it off the best they can. Thoughts such as
"Why would you hurt me? I'm not as tough as I appear!" flash
through their minds as they try to make sense of the world. I
remember, at age fourteen, wanting to just shut off my emotions
like a water faucet. But humans are not meant to be detached.

Experiments have shown lack of physical touch leads to
depression and apathy. Walk through the fire; you will be okay.
If you try to block it out, you will most likely only succeed in
building pressure that eventually needs release. But by being a
channel and allowing the pain to pass through and not attach,
just breathing through it (like in yoga), you can gain compassion and feeling. You probably are going to be a real gift to
people—helping others. First you have to help yourself. Just
because you feel fear, doesn't mean you have to be afraid of it.

Getting back to feeling begins with little steps. Let yourself feel anything you can. To rejoin the land of the living, cast this spell on the night of the new moon or on a Friday. Light a green candle. Green is the color your heart chakra (one of seven energy centers located throughout your body) resonates to. It is an auspicious or favorable place to begin a much-needed and important healing. According to *A Course in Miracles,* the most sacred of all places is where love abides where an ancient hatred once stood.

By the light of the candle, make a list on a piece of parchment paper of your favorite childhood activities, especially the silly and timeless ones. If you draw a blank, write down some of these: running through sprinklers; playing hopscotch; playing *"Twinkle, Twinkle Little Star"* or *"You Are My Sunshine"* on a musical instrument; swimming by moonlight; pasting, painting, gluing, or coloring; playing with LEGO bricks, Lincoln Logs, or Hot Wheels; eating Jell-O with your fingers; watching a Disney flick with popcorn, your favorite candy and soda; having a picnic; hiking; or rereading your favorite book.

Imagine yourself doing these activities. Fold your list and place the paper inside a green cloth, about six square inches. Now grate half of a crayon from every color of the rainbow. Mix one drop of peppermint oil, one-fourth teaspoon of ginger, and the crayon bits into the pouch.

Chant

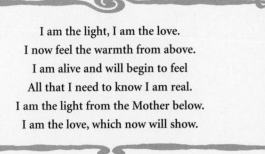

I am the light, I am the love.
I now feel the warmth from above.
I am alive and will begin to feel
All that I need to know I am real.
I am the light from the Mother below.
I am the love, which now will show.

Tie the pouch with a red ribbon, and place the pouch on your altar next to the green candle. Once you have cast the spell, reach out and literally touch your friends and family for a week. Just graze a friend's arm as you pass by, hold your parent's hands, or place your hand on your sister's or brother's arm while you talk. Come to your altar every day for a week, take three deep breaths, and repeat the chant.

HEAL FROM ILLNESS, PAIN, OR NEGATIVITY

The best time to perform this ritual is at the new moon. Take one chicken egg, which should be white, unfertile, and from a free-range chicken, if possible. Let the egg sit at room temperature for half an hour before you start. Remove your clothing and carefully roll the egg all over your body, starting at your feet. You do not have to hit every body part, but start low and end at the top of your head. If you hurt more in one particular place, spend more time rolling the egg there. You might want to do this sitting on the floor or on your bed. Take your time. Think of the egg as if it were a sponge, soaking up all the pain or illness in your body.

Understand that even if you do not know why or how you became ill, your body does. Acknowledge that your body created this disease (dis-ease) and can take it away as well. Ask your body to reverse the steps it used to bring about the pain and discomfort. Be assertive; your body listens to every word you say. When you are done, take an indelible marker and write on the egg as follows:

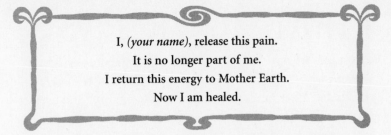

> I, *(your name)*, release this pain.
> It is no longer part of me.
> I return this energy to Mother Earth.
> Now I am healed.

You will have to write pretty small. Put the egg in a paper bag to dispose of it in a trashcan far from your home. When you are ready to throw the egg away, crush it inside the bag first, and then toss it.

HEAL YOUR PAST

Sometimes we have an acute sensitive attachment to a painful incident we have chosen to block out entirely rather than look at it again. Other times we review the incident over and over again. Regardless, if we do not let go of our painful attachment to the event, it will eventually cause us harm. The pain grows until, like a weed, it wraps around the heart and squeezes out all truth concerning similar manners.

Carrying old hurts with you is similar to living with a constant, dull pain. Granted, in shedding yourself of the painful experience, you may feel sharper and more acute tenderness, but then there will be no more grief. C. S. Lewis's *Chronicles of Narnia,* my favorite childhood series and one I still adore, used a lot of spiritual symbolism. In *The Voyage of the Dawn Treader,* Eustace had a nasty disposition. He found a dragon's cave, put on a gold arm ring, and turned into a dragon. The painful ring, which fit nicely on the arm of a boy, cut into the skin of a dragon. Aslan, the lion and representation of Spirit, told him he would have to shed his skin to release the pain. The boy peeled off layer after layer, but he was still a dragon. It wasn't until Aslan helped, reaching deeply to peel off the skin, did the healing come: "And when he began pulling the skin off, it hurt worse than anything I've ever felt. The only thing that made me able to bear it was just the pleasure of feeling the stuff peel off. . . . I found that all the pain had gone from my arm."

THE TEEN SPELL BOOK

You would be amazed to discover how many adults hold on to painful situations from the teen years that determine how they judge and respond to friends, relatives, and even strangers. If you can heal yourself of childhood hurts as well as the ones that happened recently, you will be a more confident, helpful, and open person.

You will invoke the Chinese goddess of compassion, Kwan Yin. Mix together one pound of sea salt and two drops of each of the following oils: lotus for shedding, detachment, and the past; lavender for manifestation; and frankincense and myrrh for power. Add one drop of blue food coloring, as this is a healing color. Stir in a clockwise direction and chant

I, who felt violated or hurt, am no longer that vulnerable person.
My thoughts shall no longer cause the situation to worsen.
I have moved on to embody goddess Kwan Yin of compassion,
Who holds me up and molds me in her loving fashion.

Put one tablespoon of the bath salt mixture in a lukewarm bath. Soak for at least five minutes a day for seven to nine days. Quiet your mind in a meditative trance. Each time you think of any sad or hurtful incident, place that image in a balloon in your mind's eye, and watch it fade from sight. With each bath, repeat the chant. Because this is a long chant, you may want to write it down separately and read from your note until you memorize it.

RID YOURSELF OF GUILT AND SHAME

Self-imposed guilt and shame are nasty little demons. If you are responsible for causing someone pain, especially deliberately, then you must take immediate action to correct and remedy the situation. Beyond this initial and imperative step, you must let it go. Understand that resentment has a high price tag. Holding bitter thoughts—even against yourself—takes mental, emotional, and physical energy. It makes you obsessive, angry, and depressed. These thoughts work like poison, contaminating our self-esteem and self-image with debilitating force. Challenge the "shoulds" in your thinking. Forgiveness of yourself is much easier when you give up the irrational belief that you could have done better. This only fuels your frustration, anger, and hostility. Beware of the "shoulds" in your thinking and speaking:

I should have known better.
I shouldn't act or feel that way.
I should be more attentive to my needs.
I've worked hard, and I should have been rewarded.

As the saying goes, Do not "should" on yourself. Each time you say *should,* it's as if you placed a twenty-pound weight on your shoulders. The load will not make correcting your actions any easier. You are a spiritual, privileged child of the Universe. There is no need to whip yourself into shape.

Practice this little ritual whenever you find the word *should* in your mind and speech. Hold a piece of pink rose quartz, a symbol of unconditional love, in each hand. Tell yourself it is unrealistic to expect that you will always respond in the perfect manner. Remind yourself everyone is fallible and capable of making a mistake. Whenever a hostile or hateful thought enters your mind, try to be fully aware of the harm that resentment can do to you, even making you ill. See those bitter thoughts rise out of your head like a balloon. Imagine taking a pin to the balloon and popping it—vanquishing and diffusing all its energy and power. See the words explode into a mass of confetti letters, and visually reassemble the energy as a light pink light. Watch as the pink light enters your heart center as love for yourself. Repeat this charm each time anger, shame, or guilt enters your awareness. Allow the knowledge that you are a treasured and loved child of Spirit to further motivate you to forgive and let go.

TAKE A PURIFYING BATH

After an illness or a time when things have been bad, it is a good idea to take a spiritually purifying bath. This ritual will neutralize negative influences and get you back into balance.

You will need the flower heads from eight white carnations. Light a white candle in the bathroom, and fill the tub with warm water. If you really need a shower to clean up, do it before this ritual because you will not be using any soap, bubble bath, or shampoo, just flowers and water. Toss the carnations into the water, and get into the tub. You will actually use the flowers as if they were soap, lightly scrubbing yourself with them and picturing all negativity being washed away from your body and soul. While you are doing this, you can use this incantation:

Healing power, pure and white,
Darkness be gone, let there be light!
Wash this pain away from me.
I am now whole, so Mote It Be!

THE TEEN SPELL BOOK

Remember to get your head wet too. When you are done, you may want to sit on a towel for a couple minutes to let the flower water dry on your skin. When you drain the tub, be sure to put some cheesecloth or a strainer over the drain so you don't clog up the plumbing. You can also scoop up the flowers out of the water using a mesh spaghetti strainer or colander (your parents will really appreciate it!). As the water drains out of the tub, so do all your troubles.

KNOWLEDGE AND
SELF-KNOWLEDGE
SPELLS

CULTIVATE YOUR INTUITION

To increase your intuition, it helps to cultivate your state of innocence. I do not mean naivete or inexperience. I refer to an innocence that is a suspension of disbelief, a willingness to be free of judgment, open, and incorruptible by the logical brain, which would dismiss all forms of magick, foresight, or intuition as meager chance. It is hard to make room for magick without being open to the possibility that mystical, unexplainable events occur around us every day.

Innocence encompasses a primary ingredient: trust. When you trust your instincts and follow Spirit's advice, the little voice of intuition grows stronger and clearer. It is not that your intuition develops per se, because it is always there; it is just that the channel between you and Spirit becomes less cluttered.

Cultivating your intuition begins with innocence and moves into trust. Lastly, you must clear the channel—the medium through which the message is passed.

Intuition means "inner teacher." Your inner teacher speaks to you in a quiet, guiding voice. The more you follow the direction given, the stronger your confidence will grow.

To encourage awareness of your intuition, you need to quiet the endless chatter of your mind and listen and meditate,

118

focusing on the region of your gut. To begin this meditation, set aside time when you will not be disturbed.

Burn sandalwood incense, a great scent for developing intuition. Take ten deep breaths. Do not try to resist or try to control any distracting thoughts, but allow them to surface. Then release each thought with an exhalation. Concentrate on your breathing. Listen to each breath; exhale and inhale. Then imagine yourself walking into a tiny elevator located around your heart center. Descend in the elevator until you reach your control center. This center will be where your impression and instinctive feelings about people, places, and things originate. This is the locality of the female seed of wisdom, known to the Japanese as *tang kien,* whereas the Chinese call it *dong qian.* It may differ for some, but people often find their control center under the belly button. Place your hands at this focal point. Here is your place of intuitive wisdom, where knowledge exists beyond rationality. It is a sensing of the truth, a knowing instead of thinking. Honor your body's ability to know things your mind cannot. It illustrates the difference between thinking of an idea and experiencing your understanding. When you ask a question, the answers come with feelings of calm.

If you practice this meditation for fifteen minutes every day for one week, you will begin to hear a quiet voice guiding you. As you clear the channel, your interpretation of the spiritual meaning and knowledge of how to practically apply it in the physical world will become easier and more accurately attuned to the original message.

Discover What Others Say About You

With this spell, you can know when people say flattering things about you or intercept rumors about yourself before they do any damage. One of the best things that can happen to you is to overhear someone complimenting you. Unsolicited compliments are revealing and uncensored. They expose raw feelings that show how another really sees you.

Yet when you cast this spell, you must also be prepared for whatever information comes through because this process can be misleading. Let's say you cast this spell, and now you know one of your best friends agreed with some pretty awful things someone said about you. But what if the person starting the gossip intimidated her or him? Maybe your friend will work like crazy to dispel the negativity sent your way and set the record straight. Because that type of information will not be revealed with this spell, make sure you are ready for the results of this magickal incantation.

On the night of the dark moon, light two white candles, and place them on an altar, table, or shelf. Fill a medium-sized pot with fresh springwater, and bring the water to a boil. Place two bay leaves, two tablespoons of mugwort, and two tablespoons

120

of cinquefoil (this flower is part of the rose family) in water. Cover and boil for five minutes. Transfer the pot to the altar, table, or shelf, placing it on a safe trivet or wooden hot pad. Remove the lid and breathe in the fragrant steam. Relax your mind and chant quietly:

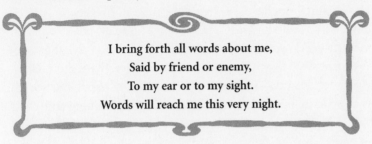

I bring forth all words about me,
Said by friend or enemy,
To my ear or to my sight.
Words will reach me this very night.

Concentrate on your breathing as you chant.

DISCOVER YOUR UNIQUE GIFT

How many times have you heard the phrase "Everybody has a gift"? This would be great news if only you knew what your gift is, what makes *you* special. It may be quite obvious what gifts your friends, parents, brothers, or sisters were given, but now you have begun to wonder if you stood in the wrong line while waiting to be born. If you got a gift, where is it hiding and would it please come out, because you have gotten pretty tired of being so completely ordinary?

It is true that everyone on earth was given a special talent, a gift. It is not just a mantra repeated by exceptional people who took pity on you. You might just need a little help uncovering it.

Perform this spell the night after the new moon. While the moon is waxing to fullness, you will call on the Crone goddess Hecate. The reason you will invoke the sagacious and wise elder is because she embodies experience. Hecate has been around for some time; she has seen your gift and knows how to help you discover, cultivate, and use it well. Anoint a black witch candle and bloodstone gem with Hecate oil and blessing oil. As you rub on the oil, say

Hecate, old and wise, powerful and true,
Help me see the gift that is my due.
Empower me to use it with good intent,
So all may benefit from my talent.

Repeat the ritual for three consecutive nights. Carry the stone with you until you feel you have successfully discovered your talent and have obtained the knowledge of how to use it wisely.

FIND OUT IF YOU LEAD OR FOLLOW

If you could place the teen years along the line of the chakra system, they would vacillate between the second and third chakras. The second chakra is the center of the harmonizing of your polar opposites. It is the place of sex, power, and money. Here resonates your drive, ambition, and desire to accumulate things. Without a strong connection to this chakra, you will feel unprotected and ungrounded. The third chakra known as the solar plexus is the center of your foundation and will. Here you may find out where you belong and why.

You might consider yourself fully rooted in either a leader or follower position, or you may see yourself as someone who floats between the two roles. The world needs both commanders and soldiers, masters and disciples. As long as you know why you are situated in your role, all is well. But I ask you to challenge the reasoning behind your placement.

The more you use divination to interpret your motivation and choices in life, the more you will move into a calm stillness. Soon you will learn to detach yourself from the outcome and your perception will enlarge as you can now see your problems from a distance. This is called being the witness or silent observer.

From this stillness you will be able to match the situation against the Divine order, not just the rigidity and permanence

124

of society's value system. Examples of this thinking and courage are seen from Christianity to Wicca. When the merchants were charging double for taxes, Jesus went in their marketplace and overturned their tables, putting a stop to this business practice. According to Italian Wicca, Aradia fought all convention by bringing the wisdom of her teachings to humans for their spiritual evolution.

These examples not only point to how to determine the validity of the roles we play in groups of friends, but it also pertains to what causes and ideas we support. Learn to think for yourself. If you are unclear about your motivations, try this ritual.

Hang a clear quartz crystal (one that has been blessed with saltwater and has lain in the light of the full moon) from a cord, chain, or piece of leather. Hold the end perfectly still, and ask Spirit if your motivations regarding your troubled situation are pure. Concentrate on your question, and then let go of the pendulum. If it swings in a linear fashion, either back and forth or from side to side, the answer is no. If it swings in a circular manner, the answer is yes. You can determine the reasons you act in or believe certain ways by continuing to ask yes or no questions. Be sure to hold the thought firmly in your mind before you let go of the pendulum. Getting the right or needed answers from Spirit begins with asking specific and hard questions.

FIND YOUR ANIMAL TOTEM

You may already have a clue about your animal totem or spirit guide. There may be an animal you have always loved and to which you have felt a special connection. This could be a cat, a lion, a wolf, a dolphin, an eagle, a hummingbird, a pig, or a frog. It could also be a mythical beast, such as a dragon or unicorn. If you are already drawn to a specific animal, you may have already unconsciously chosen your animal guide, or it may have chosen you. Think about the qualities this creature possesses. How can this animal teach you? What gifts of the animal would you like to emulate?

If you don't feel a kinship with a certain animal, or you're just not sure, don't worry. Before you go to bed, take a notebook or dream journal, and write this incantation:

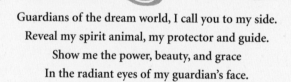

Guardians of the dream world, I call you to my side.
Reveal my spirit animal, my protector and guide.
Show me the power, beauty, and grace
In the radiant eyes of my guardian's face.

Use this incantation or your own words to let the guardians of the dream world know you are ready to meet your spirit animal guide. Be patient: It might not happen the first night, so keep trying. Eventually, you will have a dream in which your animal totem appears—and you might be surprised which animal shows up! One very petite and quiet girl I know found out her spirit guide animal was a huge male mountain gorilla. Most animals have strengths and lessons they can lend us, and most people will carry more than one medicine from the animal kingdom. Sometimes you will consistently run into or across a particular animal.

Once you find out which animal you belong with, you might wish to get a picture of it for your room, or maybe some jewelry or a T-shirt with the animal's image, to remind you of your special magickal relationship. Your animal can be called on to help you in the dream world or give you strength in times of need. Just picture the animal in your mind. For additional information on animal totems, refer to page 52.

(Victoria Bearden, astrologer, psychic, and magickal practitioner, generously offered this spell.)

FIND YOUR CAREER PATH

In an age in which work is such a central point of life for most of us, finding the right career is critical to the overall enjoyment of life. Following a magickal path puts us in touch with the infinite creative energy of the Universe and gives us access to manifesting that energy in our own lives. While it is exciting and useful to have the skills to "manifest" those exact things we want, it is also important to remember that sometimes, when we "run the show" in these manifestations, we may limit ourselves and the outcomes. We certainly can tell Spirit what we want, visualize it, and materialize it through various practices and rituals, but truly magickal people realize the perfect order in the consciousness that lives beyond our reach. With that in mind, the following meditation is designed to tap into our creative power while still honoring the perfect order of the Great Mystery. This is a lengthy meditation that you will most likely want to tape yourself.

Sit in a comfortable position, and focus your attention on your breath. Breathe long and deep on the inhalation, and relax on the exhalation, entirely to its own rhythm. Visualize with each inhalation a deep green light filling you. As the light fills your body and begins to spill outward, allow it to become a bubble of light, in which you sit. Watch as the bubble lifts off

the ground, floating up and out of your house or wherever you are with you in it. Let your bubble carry you to an unknown destination. When you begin to feel the bubble set down, ask Spirit (by whatever name works for you) to blow a breeze upon you, which clears your body and mind of any preconceived ideas about what your career or job should look like. Feel the wind blow across and through you; feel the magickal breeze lift away any residue of control about your career issue, regardless of how that may or may not match your own ideas. With this consciousness in place, allow yourself to step out of the bubble, examine your surroundings, and see yourself in a beautiful outdoor garden with a magickal labyrinth to walk.

Notice there is only one destination in the labyrinth, even though it turns and bends. Visualize seven different spots along the labyrinth walk where small altars rest. As you approach the first, leave on the altar a talent or gift you feel you have to share with the world. Once you have one in mind, write it on a piece of paper and wrap a ribbon around it. Place it on the altar as a gift. Continue on your walk, and as you approach the second altar, notice that it has a gift for you. Keep an open mind about what you see there. It might be a gift that is symbolic, one that you will recognize the meaning of later. Take the gift and hold it as you continue on your walk. Continue your walk until you reach the third altar. On this altar, there is a Zen "sand" garden and a feather. Using the feather, draw a complete circle in the sand, and write the word *job* or *career* in the center. Place in the center the gift you received at the previous altar. As you walk farther and approach the fourth altar, notice that it has photos of all the important people in your life, including a portrait of you. Here, offer a prayer that your career be one that harmoniously honors the lifestyle and needs of all the people you love, including yourself. At the next altar down the path, notice that there is a small bench, a fruit tree, a small shovel, watering can, and a scroll and pen. The scroll is for you to write down all the things you love to do in life. Visualize yourself writing the list with anything that comes to mind, even those things that seem unrelated to a job or career. Beneath the fruit tree, use the shovel to bury the scroll, and water the area thoroughly. Know that the energy of this list will become part of the tree and will eventually come to fruition. Wander the labyrinth farther, and at the sixth altar, notice a magickal window, in which different pictures present themselves for your review as you gaze out. Ask Spirit to show you anything pertinent about your perfect job or career. Stay out of your rational mind, and observe whatever you see without judgment. When you are ready, finish your labyrinth walk at the final altar in its center. At this altar is an appointment book. Write your name in the book, with a commitment to accept your perfect career. Notice that this book has no time or dates. Allow Spirit to work on it's own timetable, knowing that our ultimate "big picture" requirements may differ from what we think our earthly timetable is. Be open. When you are ready, come back to your green bubble, and let it carry you back to your pre-meditation spot. Open your eyes and feel your Spirit reenter your body, coming fully back to your present surroundings. Be sure to make notes of any information, symbols, and so on that the meditation provided.

Now that you have called the perfect career forth at the inner level, your work is to show up for life. Go to interviews or take prerequisite classes to move you in the direction of your perfect career, let people know you are looking and open, and allow Spirit to deliver your job to you. Trust that it will happen. I always use the prayer, "May Spirit close any doors to me that do not serve my highest good to walk through, and let Spirit roll a red carpet before me to show me what direction to go." The most important thing is to trust the magickal process and stay out of your linear mind. Do the footwork, but let Spirit bring the outcome. Know that Spirit will bring you the career that best serves your completion or coming full circle on your path to spiritual enlightenment and realization.

SEE THE FUTURE

When we see into the future, we are presented with possibilities. It is our choice to determine how we want to experience these life lessons or situations.

During a book signing for *The Wicca Cookbook,* which was held before I had begun to write this book, a woman in the audience told me I would get the contract for a teen book. A Wiccan High Priestess and proprietor of the Rose and Chalice Web site (see Resource Guide), she foresaw that I would go through a rite of passage during the writing process. It was a necessary sloughing off of old thought patterns that no longer served me. What she did not try to predict was what it would be like for me. The removal of this unnecessary skin was inevitable. How attached I was to that ego or perception of myself would determine whether my experience would be liberating or painful.

Whether you are paying for someone else to foretell your future or decide to utilize your own psychic powers, the information you receive needs to work as a guiding tool. You are being offered choices of different alternative routes, side roads. The information is offered for you to accept or reject. It may be revealed to you that patterns could repeat or there exists an end that you must achieve for spiritual development but the path you choose to walk is up to you.

Reading the future can be accomplished by many different means. You can use a variety of divination tools to help you focus and bring out your own clairvoyance, which is also

132

known as the Sight. You can use tarot cards, a pendulum, a dark pool or body of water, dowsing rods, rune stones, or any tools of your own design. Perform this ritual three nights after the dark moon, because it is the time to divine the unseen forces at work in your life.

Take ten deep breaths. Clear your mind of all thoughts; focus on your breathing. Burn a yellow candle for mental clarity and a white candle for pure intent. Burn incense of any of these scents: patchouli, cinnamon, or sandalwood. Rinse a clear quartz crystal with seawater or saltwater, and pass your crystal through the incense smoke. Set the crystal on a special cloth in the light of the moon. Say

> I now invoke thee, O Mother of mine,
> To tell my tale with this crystal of thine.
> Help me to see with your pure Divine light
> Whether my future is dark or bright.

Concentrate on your breathing and follow with your mind's eye any symbols you see. Do not try to analyze now, just watch the images and listen.

SEE THE FAERIES

If seeing is believing, then believing begins with acknowledging. You are divinely a cocreator of everything that comes into your life. All of creation begins with a thought, then the word is spoken, and last the image takes form in matter. The same goes with faeries. They exist in their shimmering world but will appear in ours when asked.

Faeries love to play, but they like to be invited. They are delighted to make friends with humans, just as you will be tickled to have the little imps, dryads, and elves on your side. Try this spell every day for one week, though sprite-like appearances may happen well before the week is out. You may find that mushrooms spring up, flickers of light stream just in corner of your eye, you hear twinkles of laughter, bells rings, and the faeries might pinch your nose or leave marks on the ground from their dancing and revelry.

Prepare a very sweet dessert, preferably something with cream or honey in it. As you bake, play faery music, if you have any; otherwise, intermittently ring bells or chimes. It is okay to get the cookies, treats, or cakes from the grocery store, just do so with the intent of giving them to the faeries. At sunrise or sunset take your treats, along with a sprig of wild thyme, outside to your backyard. Another great time to do this is on the evening of Beltane. If you do not have a backyard, go to a place in nature such as a park or even to a window box of flowers. Ring bells or chimes and say

134

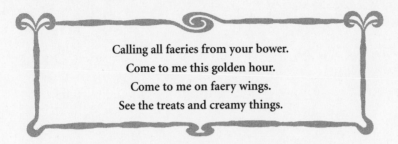

Calling all faeries from your bower.
Come to me this golden hour.
Come to me on faery wings.
See the treats and creamy things.

Close your eyes, place the thyme over your dominant eye, and while repeating the chant, move in the direction you feel the strongest vibration of light and playful energy. As you leave your treat for the faeries, you can either talk to them or just walk away.

When my son, Skyler, and I left food (quartered blueberry bagels with whipped cream and honey) for the faeries this Beltane I saw and felt them gather around my bed that night. They shook my outstretched hand, laughed, and gave heart-felt thanks for being acknowledged.

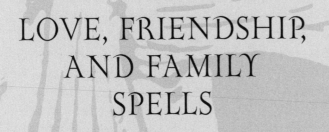

LOVE, FRIENDSHIP,
AND FAMILY
SPELLS

BANISH LONELINESS

You may have difficulty making friends or the friends you have do not fill your companionship needs. Regardless of who you meet it feels like no one understands you, nor you them. The problem may lie in a restrictive or exclusionary attitude. The first step to combating loneliness is an openness and willingness to see any similarities between you and possible friends. The people in your immediate environment are there for a reason: to teach lessons to you or receive lessons from you.

It may also feel like you have grown apart from even your best of friends. Much of the spiritual path is letting go of the need to change others. It is through letting go of trying to keep others from growing that we can truly embrace what is real. Alone time can be this way too. Sometimes being in a crowd and feeling no one sees you is the loneliest feeling of all. Cultivate alone time and do not be afraid of the stillness. Make time to meditate. Get away from electricity and be still. In this space you will feel a connection to everyone.

Cast this spell on a Sunday. Gather several empty paper towel or toilet paper holder and different colored plastic wrap. Cover each holder at one end with one color, and bind it with a rubber band. Look through your colored "telescopes" at a clear crystal. Notice how the crystal looks different each time. The

138

seer is the same source, you, but the reflection is different depending on the lens. This illustrates how your reality can change, depending on your frame of reference. Sprinkle one-half teaspoon of sea salt in a vessel of water. Say

> By the pure element of salt,
> I clear this water of former energy.

Ring a bell and place the crystal in the water. Add a rose quartz crystal (representing friendship). Sprinkle one-half teaspoon of nutmeg and one-half teaspoon of cloves into the water. Drop in four sunflower seeds. Say the following chant three times

> I now release the idea that I am lonely,
> Calling forth friends in good company.
> By the seeds, spices, and crystals there,
> I bring in friends and good times to share.

ESTABLISH TRUST WITH YOUR PARENTS

To get your parents to relax a little, you have to earn their trust and learn compromise. You need to convince them you are trustworthy and able to handle responsibilities, such as more use of the family car, a later curfew, or your own phone. Sometimes parents get so busy in their lives, they forget you have changed and grown. It is not that they intend to ignore you, it is just that most of us are preoccupied by the fast pace of our own lives. You can understand this concept if you ever assumed your best friend's favorite color was yellow, just to find out they changed it to blue six months ago.

Set up a meeting to discuss all your new accomplishments and the responsibilities you have carried over the past year. Give specific examples of why you need some rules changed. For example, you need more use of the family car to get to work or gymnastic practice. Be ready to compromise; if your parents will not budge, offer to find alternative means of getting to work for two weeks, and then set a date to renegotiate. When you do get to drive the car, keep the car clean, put even a couple of bucks worth of gas in the tank, and drive responsibly.

THE TEEN SPELL BOOK

Set the meeting for a Monday. This day rules the home and family, and it is under the influence of the moon, which brings about subtle changes. Be sure the time is convenient for both your parents. The spell will have an overall better effect for you if they are both there, even if they don't live together.

You will call on the assistance of the Egyptian goddess Hathor. While Hathor rules music and dancing, she also has the ability to infuse responsibility into you and allow parents to trust you. This spell will be cast over the room in which the meeting will take place, not your parents. You want to infuse a sense of open-mindedness and increase the possibility for positive opportunities. Prepare the room the night before your meeting. Light a sage bundle, and blow out the flame, allowing the dry leaves to ember. With a turkey feather or your hand, direct the smoke into all corners of the room. Say

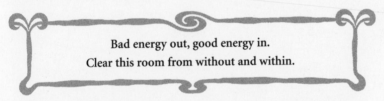

Bad energy out, good energy in.
Clear this room from without and within.

After you have cleared the room of its former energy, burn a stick of sandalwood incense for success. Light a blue candle for truth and a purple candle for Divine order. Beginning in the east, draw a pentagram with either your athame or finger in every direction. Say

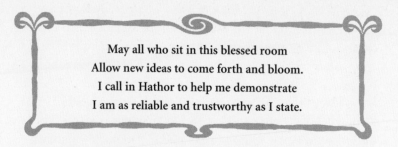

May all who sit in this blessed room
Allow new ideas to come forth and bloom.
I call in Hathor to help me demonstrate
I am as reliable and trustworthy as I state.

Leave either lavender, sunflower, or violet flowers in the center of the room. All these flowers symbolize wishes and their successful manifestation.

Find How You Fit In

Almost everyone has a strong desire to feel they belong. It is natural to want to feel you are part of a community or group. As souls, we are all connected to Spirit, so there is no separation of anyone on that level. And we are all different. The way we describe a sunset, a night out, the flu, cold weather, our fears, dreams, hopes, and how we perceive love is so very different.

The path to fitting in begins with cultivating and nurturing your uniqueness. There is a dynamic, a group with an empty round hole with special features, distinctions, and nuances, waiting for you that will perfectly embrace your round peg with its idiosyncrasies, quirks, and habits. Of course, this is an oversimplification, but there exists a group that needs what you can offer. Until you know what your gifts and contributions are, you cannot very well offer them. For example, maybe you are a born leader or a good listener. Perhaps you are just funky or daring enough to suggest things this group never thought they could enjoy, but they would just flourish under the new ideas and experiences.

Pay attention to your likes and dislikes; try not to imagine or associate with any one group as you do this. Write down all your qualities on a piece of parchment paper. This process will draw you to attract or pull you toward the right group for you. Bless the paper by wafting incense of frankincense and myrrh over it. Say

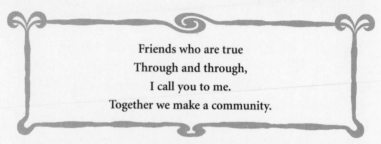

Friends who are true
Through and through,
I call you to me.
Together we make a community.

Leave the paper on your altar or bury under your favorite tree or plant (this does not need to be in your own backyard).

FIND LOVE

Love spells are tricky work. At one time or another, we all have had our eyes on the perfect guy or gal for us, or so we think. The problem is we do not always see the whole picture; maybe he or she is the one, and maybe he or she is not. Regardless, there can be no denying it: Being with a special person feels awesome. It is wonderful to share good times and see him or her look at you in that way that makes your knees melt into gelatin and your stomach do so many flips you think you will never eat again.

Spells should not be cast on or over someone else. When you cast this spell, you will be trying to manifest love to come into your life. There is nothing the matter with hoping the one you have a crush on will be Mr. or Ms. Right, but Spirit may have a better plan. Always remember that you need to be confident in yourself and not to put your hopes on any guy or girl just to fill emptiness inside.

Cast this spell on a Friday morning close to or on a full moon. Before the dew has evaporated, take the petals from a rose, preferably a pink or red rose. If you do not have roses in your garden, buy a rose and leave it outside overnight. Take a pink piece of cloth about four inches in diameter, and place just the petals inside. Dab a bit of gardenia, rose, or lavender oil behind your ears. When the full moon rises, rinse a piece of rose quartz in saltwater and say

> I cleanse and infuse this stone
> For my energy alone.
> Bring me the love I desire
> By the will of our higher power.

Place the stone in the cloth. Bind the cloth with a red string or ribbon. As you do this, chant

> Aphrodite, your power of love divine,
> Bring me a love that is mine.
> Bring him (her) to me in perfect trust.
> Harm to none is a must.

Carry the pouch with you always. Even sleep with it under your pillow. When a new love enters your life, bury the pouch under your favorite flower, bush, or tree. Then follow up with the Give Thanks for Love spell on page 149.

Note: You may choose to substitute Aphrodite with the male god Adonis.

Find a True
Friend

Jan was probably one of my truest friends when I was fifteen.
There was no pretending or competition in our friendship. We
had different interests and were open-minded and accepting of
someone from whom we had so much to learn. This simple
acceptance and lack of judgment allowed me to risk and be
whomever I wanted or needed to be. Because she offered such a
tolerance for my quirkiness, I sought to return her gift.

A true friend doesn't put what they gain by being with you
ahead of what they can offer you. Sometimes life itself appears
to be one big competition: to get the guy or girl, the job, or the
lead in the school play or band. When you use a bird's-eye view
and distance yourself from sweating the small stuff, you begin
to get a glimpse that we are all one big family, here to help one
another. To find a true friend, you must first be a true friend.

What matters in this life is more than winning for ourselves.
What matters is helping others win, even if it means slowing
down and changing our course. A candle loses nothing by
lighting another candle.

Cast this spell on a Sunday, the day of friendship. Choose a
candle of your favorite color, and anoint it with your favorite
scent, whether it is a perfume, cologne, oil, or flower essence.
Light the candle and encircle it with your favorite symbols and

images; these can include pictures of yourself, especially those taken in your favorite places or with a particular smile or expression you like. Cup your hands about six inches in front of the candle. Send your energy to the flame of that candle as if you were feeding it your light. Say

> By the hermetic law of similarity,
> This candle now represents my personality.

Take a yellow candle (yellow because it is akin to the sun and representative of Sunday), and hold it in your hands. Say

> By the hermetic law of similarity,
> This candle now represents a friend's personality.

Take your candle and light the yellow candle. Say

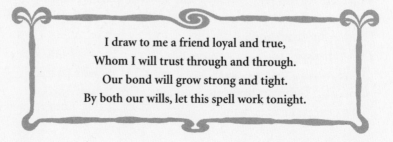

> I draw to me a friend loyal and true,
> Whom I will trust through and through.
> Our bond will grow strong and tight.
> By both our wills, let this spell work tonight.

GIVE THANKS
FOR LOVE

Attracting love is so important, especially during the teen years.
Love spells are the most requested and most often used. In
adherence to the Wiccan tradition of giving thanks when you
have asked for assistance, I offer this ritual of gratitude. The
love spell listed on page 145 calls on Aphrodite's assistance. If
you chose to substitute Venus, then make the appropriate
substitution here.

Cast this spell on a Friday during any phase of the moon, as
long as it is visible. Use a burin, engraving tool, or other device
to inscribe a white image candle with your name and any other
personal symbols. Anoint the candle with your astrological oil
and place it where it can receive the light of the moon. Light a
stick of dove's blood, Aphrodite, or Venus incense. Dove's blood
is not actually made from the blood of a dove, but has been
given this name to illustrate its gentle healing and loving
properties. Light two pink candles, representing you and your
new love, and place them on either side of your white image
candle. Look up at the moon and say

Aphrodite, goddess of love,
I honor and thank you
For this gift from above.
Blessings on your name and heart.
Merry meet and merry part.

If possible and safe, allow the candles to burn out. You may need to transfer them to your altar.

HAVE A PEACEFUL BREAKUP

This spell is designed to work for a breakup you know is coming, and it can work for a boyfriend, girlfriend, or just a friend. You may be anxious about causing hurt feelings, burning a bridge, or bringing on a strong, even violent, reaction. Maybe you have even put off separating from this person because of your perception of what may happen.

Most likely, their attitude and disposition have given you reason to be nervous, but you do not need to focus on them. Whatever you focus on will grow. Each time you imagine a dramatic scene taking place, it is as if you are fertilizing a plant with your "crappy" thoughts. So even if it seems absolutely impossible, begin to visualize a smooth breakup and either a transition into a new level of friendship or a complete separation.

This spell has two parts. You will call on Kali, the goddess of death, destruction, and rebirth. She is very powerful, so concentrate on her ability to help you separate, as well as her strength in rebuilding. The wild boar also helps with confrontation and gives you strength to stand your ground. Once you have gained the chutzpah or guts to face the breakup, then you need to balance and temper it with compassion. The reason you are separating from this person is they no longer have gifts to offer you. Their way works for them, not you, so there is still something worth honoring. For this idea, we will call in Kwan Yin and deer medicine, both of which will help you gain a gentle force and fortitude.

Light an orange candle. Hold two pieces of black tourmaline or onyx in each hand. Visualize a yellowish orange fire building in your belly. Focus on all the reasons you need to part from this person. Imagine Kali and the wild boar standing behind you as you hold your position. Hold these thoughts for at least ten minutes. You do not have to stand perfectly still for this part of the ritual. It may work best to pace or involve some kind of movement as you build your strength.

Then sit down and light a blue candle. Imagine Kwan Yin and the deer in all their gentle strength. With fluidity, they can shape-shift a tumultuous event into a calm, soothing parting. Understand that both of you have reasons for the way you are and that neither are right or wrong. Imagine the separation without drama. You do not have to divulge every reason for parting as long as you keep your integrity. Hold these thoughts for ten calm minutes. You may want to include gentle, swaying movements.

Now take ten deep breaths and say

I part from you this very day,
Releasing you to be in your own way.
Thank you for the gifts you gave.
May our paths be blessed, good-bye I wave.

Go outside and throw the two pieces of black tourmaline or onyx in opposite directions.

Note: This was by far the hardest spell to write and one of the last ones to come forth—until I had to face it in life. The idea that I did not know how to say good-bye without burning a bridge became a piece of luggage that I was finally ready to drop. I have confidence this spell will work for you as smoothly as it did for me and will be as uplifting.

Heal a Broken Heart

Heartbreak often takes us by surprise. When we see a breakup coming, we can brace ourselves and begin letting go in small increments. It is the breakups that come out of nowhere that shatter our confidence and sense of security. In this spell, we will concentrate on releasing the painful experience and building a new foundation for you.

Diana is the perfect aspect of the Goddess to call on to rescue your broken heart. Because of her assertiveness and independence, she can be invoked for healing by guys and girls equally. Diana's power and confidence are unsurpassed in the Roman pantheon. Whether you choose to seek another partner or remain single for a while, one thing is certain: You are being asked by the Universe to see the world alone again, for whatever amount of time. Diana's strength and grace will propel you toward confidence. She will help you nourish your own soul as you hunt for the new you. Her association with the moon will help you make this a subtle, gentle transition as well.

This spell will work best if you can get in Diana's backyard: the woods, forests, or at least by a grove of trees. Cast this spell on a Monday. Although there will be things you want to remember about your lost love some things need to be released before you can heal your heart. Find a symbol of something that brings you a particularly strong amount of pain. For example, this could be a card professing undying love and loyalty just before she got caught with your best friend or the plans made just before he dropped you, or a picture of the two of you or just him or her. If you cannot think of a representation, that is okay. Instead, take a piece of red carnelian and squeeze it to infuse all your heartache into the stone. Obtain a moonstone gem, walnut, a tree seedling that can grow in the area of your spell or wildflower seeds, and a watering can full of water. Next, on a piece of parchment paper, write a letter to your ex-girlfriend or ex-boyfriend. Include all the things that caused you pain and any hurtful things you did not get to say. Sprinkle two drops of camphor oil on the letter. Dig a hole big enough for your seedling or seeds, the symbol, the letter, stone(s), and walnut. Place all your items in the earth and say

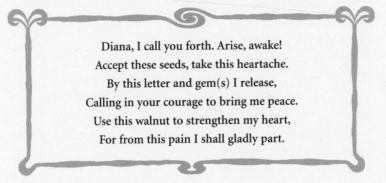

Diana, I call you forth. Arise, awake!
Accept these seeds, take this heartache.
By this letter and gem(s) I release,
Calling in your courage to bring me peace.
Use this walnut to strengthen my heart,
For from this pain I shall gladly part.

Cover with dirt and water.

HELP A FRIEND IN PAIN

This spell needs to be cast with the purest intent and with an emphasis on what is right for your friend. Sometimes we have horrible experiences so we can learn a lesson, such as how to protect, love, and honor life and ourselves. Sometimes we need to visit the edge before we can see how far down it is to fall. This spell, which will be more like a ritual prayer, can be cast for anyone who is using drugs or alcohol, is running with the wrong crowd, has bulimia or anorexia, cuts him or herself, is being hurt by another, or who has other needs.

The first thing for you to realize is your friend is the only one who can raise herself or himself out of the pain. Your job is to be supportive and unconditionally loving. Your friend is hurting, and sometimes a person's way of dealing with pain will be to lash out or even clam up; most of these actions are survival skills he or she has learned to cope and have nothing to do with you. As a friend, you are not required to sit by and be their punching bag, and do not take it personally. Before doing this spell, be sure to ask your friend's permission to make him or her a healing pouch, as magick is never performed for someone without their knowledge or permission.

Write down your friend's name on a piece of paper. Write down every wonderful quality about your friend, especially

156

those present when she or he is well. Fold the paper and place it in a green cloth. Add a piece of amethyst to your pouch. Lastly, place eucalyptus leaves or oil in the pouch. As you bind the pouch with a silver or green ribbon, say

Guardians, protect _____ (friend's name).
Right action takes place.
Help _____ (friend's name) out of this space.
Show her/him the love around
By Divine will from sky to ground.

Give the healing pouch to your friend.

MAKE PEACE WITH YOUR SIBLINGS

We are all sons and daughters of the Goddess. Some see the ocean as Her physical embodiment or incarnation. That would make each of us her little waves. Each wave moves in rhythm with the other waves, sometimes big and sometimes small. Sometimes the waves flow deep onto the sand; other times they recede into Mother Ocean herself. Their size depends on the energy behind them and the pull of Sister Moon. Regardless, there always exists the harmony.

Sometimes, as with lagoons and tide pools, the water rushes back toward the sea and collides with the incoming waves. The resulting water shoots into the air, rainbows shimmering and reflecting through the tiny droplets like a million miniature diamonds. Imagine your sibling(s) and yourself to be these two opposing waves. You have similarities: Both come from the same source, and your makeup is somewhat alike. But your direction, how you respond to life, and your course are different. When you clash, it is spectacular, or at least loud. But if all beings in the world were exactly the same, no new creations would ever be made and nothing could be gained. We would all be carbon copies of one another, and life would be disgustingly boring.

158

Perform this ritual during a waning moon, preferably on a Sunday. Fill two glasses with pure water. Put two drops of orange blossom oil in one and two drops of vanilla oil in the other (alternatively, you can use rose oil, bergamot oil, or lemon oil). Pour the two glasses of scented water into a bowl, preferably something special to both of you (such as the family popcorn bowl). As you combine the water, say

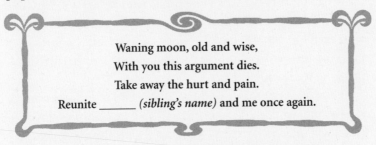

Waning moon, old and wise,
With you this argument dies.
Take away the hurt and pain.
Reunite _____ *(sibling's name)* and me once again.

Pour some of the combined water into a glass or your cauldron, and place it on your altar. Take the remaining water, and dump it in your yard, possibly near a favorite spot you share with your sister or brother. Wash the bowl.

Make Up with Friends

Part of being a teenager is formulating or bringing into form or matter the person you are and having the courage to stand up for what you believe. As we determine who we are and who we are not, this will inevitably cause a clash of ideas and direction with even our best friends. But fighting—or Goddess forbid, breaking up—with your best friend is agonizingly harder than breaking it off with a crush.

Pink is the color of unconditional love and represents friends, so anything you can do to bring more of the color into this ritual will only make the spell stronger. Unconditional love is free, unrestricted, total, and sad to say, not often felt.

On a Sunday, light a pink candle. Have three ribbons: one of your favorite color, one of your friend's favorite color, and a pink ribbon. Braid the ribbons and chant

_____ *(friend's name)* **knows me complete.**
She (He) knows my strengths and where I am weak.
Together we are bound to be as one.
Soon we will have magickal fun.

Visualize a pink light surrounding the two of you. Focus on the energy of friendship. Remember spells are not to be cast on or over someone. Mix one-fourth teaspoon of each of these spices: allspice, ground cloves, and nutmeg. Sprinkle the mixture over the braid. Leave the braid on a pink or white cloth.

Meet a Famous Person

Celebrities have stuck to their goals, be it sports, art, music, or otherwise. Through their persistence and determination, they have endured tutors and coaches, endless practice, and insane schedules. They have their weak moments, insecurities, and bad habits, just like the rest of us. The difference may be that when they fall down, they pick themselves up again. They keep their focus in mind, no matter how ridiculous it may seem to their friends and family. Celebrities hold their goals close to their hearts, and that is where they nurture and keep their desires safe.

Famous people are to be admired for their unyielding willpower. Some are even blessed people who show the world what good can be done with money and power. They donate time and financial resources, which is even more admirable than the rest. These are the true role models.

Plan to make a trip to a movie or television studio tour. Gather pictures of celebrities, preferably your favorite ones. Set them on your altar, and light an orange candle. Focus on the flame. Let your eyes blur a little, like when you are trying to see the image in a 3-D hologram. Imagine a white golden light entering through the top of your head and traveling down your body, through your toes and into the core of the earth.

Turn your focus to the pictures or names of the celebrities on your altar. Visualize actually meeting them as if you already have and these events have already happened. Consider the questions you would ask him or her, or if all you want to do is just hang out with her or him, visualize the two of you talking in a friendly, relaxed way. Feel your excitement as you speak with them as well as have a photo taken with them. Most important for the completion of this spell is to travel to a studio tour or local celebrity hangout to increase your work!

SUMMON A LOVED ONE'S SPIRIT

People come into our lives for a reason, a season, or a lifetime. Those who cross our paths for a short time often give us a gift by leaving us. In this way, their message is imprinted on our hearts like footprints in the sand, never to be erased by time or memory. We are blessed with many people in our lives, and even though some of them have died, we can still talk to or be with them.

Most of the time this connection will not be in the form of having a chat with our loved one sitting at the end of our bed, although it can be. Often what happens is that we will experience his or her presence. The room may turn cold, the wind might pick up unexpectedly, we may be surrounded in an aura of color, or animals with peculiar faces may cross our paths. Since we are all energy, even in spirit form, often our loved ones communicate with us through electricity. Lights may flicker, computers might randomly turn on, or the phone will ring but no one answers. A great time to do this spell is on Halloween, also known as Samhain; otherwise, cast this spell on a Saturday.

THE TEEN SPELL BOOK

Place a picture of your loved one on a north-facing wall, or if you can, position an altar in this direction. Light a white candle. If you know your loved one's favorite scent, either burn that incense, wear the perfume, or place the flower on the altar. If you do not know his or her favorite scent, either gather lavender sprigs, wear a few drops of the oil, or burn it as incense or oil. Light another candle of your loved one's favorite color and place it on the altar. Prepare a snack for the two of you (or however many people are in the ritual), making sure to include your loved one's favorite foods. Sit in front of your altar, and imagine her or him sitting next to you. Relax; you are only calling on the spirit of a loved one. This is called a "dumb supper." Watch for any little sign, which may also come later in a dream.

UNITE YOUR FAMILY

When your parents' relationship is strong, the base of your family life is formidable. When their relationship is rocky, it is like pillars giving way to an earthquake; the whole building sways and lurches, threatening to tear apart. Even if you are used to your parents fighting all the time, it wears away at your peace of mind, something the majority of us would have over all other spiritual gifts.

To bring peace and harmony to your home, offer to make dinner for the family, and this means *all* the family. Plan dinner for Monday, but be sure it is convenient for everyone. Monday is dedicated to home and family as it derived its name from Moon Day and the moon is sacred to women, keepers of the hearth and home. When it is needed immediately, any day will do. You can either choose to make a favorite family recipe or a basic dish of spaghetti. Try to use basil in your dish, as this herb carries with it a vibration of sympathy. This spell will not be cast *over* your parents, but will be cast to infuse peace and harmony in your home with the hope, desire, and intent of asking your parents to accept the new energy level.

Before sunrise on the day of your big dinner, sprinkle cumin seed over each doorway. While you prepare the dish, ask to be left alone. Light a long-lasting pink candle (for unconditional love), and place it in the east (the direction of air, communication, and new beginnings). Anoint your wrists with benzoin oil to infuse an energy that clears the air. While you cook, repeat

Bring to our family
Peace and harmony.

Take your pink candle to the dinner table. If it is possible, burn a sage bundle. Light one end and let the fire burn out. Direct the smoke all around the room. This act of smudging clears, purifies, and protects. Decorate the table with red or pink roses. Alternatively, anoint the tablecloth, place mats, or napkins with rose- or jasmine-scented oil. You've done the best you can. Even the effort of the dinner, regardless of the spell, should melt the hearts of your parents. Be sure to offer to clean up, and insist they sit together and talk.

MONEY
SPELLS

FEEL RICH

Money makes us feel rich. We use it as exchange for our needs and wants. Sometimes what we need can be brought to us by a gift or other simple exchange. Money is energy, just like electricity, and can come to you in many forms. Abundance is always available to you. Decide in which aspect of your life you want to feel rich. For example, do you always want to have a couple bucks in your wallet to feel secure? Do you want money for clothes, dates, or a new bicycle? Visualizing how you plan on using the money will help this spell be more successful. Remember that the money may not come to you in the form you thought it would, but you might still get the desired result, which means the spell worked.

Cast this spell on a Thursday, which is a great day for money matters. Obtain a gold or green beeswax candle sheet. Put one-half teaspoon of poppy seeds and one-half teaspoon of whole cloves in your mortar and pestle. Grind the herbs and chant

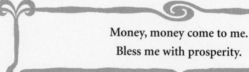

Money, money come to me.
Bless me with prosperity.

Sprinkle the herbs on the flat piece of beeswax. Imbed them into the sheet but not so much that you distort the sheet. Wrap the candle sheet, repeating the chant. Inscribe the money

symbol ($) into your candle. Anoint it with two drops of two of
these oils: mint, bergamot, bayberry, or almond. Rub one drop
of each oil on the palms of your hands. Leave the candle on
your altar.

SHOW ME THE MONEY!

This spell is for those times when you need an exact amount of money. Bartering is not going to do it. You need cash.

Cast the spell on a Thursday, which is ruled by Jupiter, who oversees wealth and material gain. The optimum time of day to perform this ritual is six hours after sunrise.

Light a green candle. On a piece of parchment paper, write in dragon's blood ink or with a gold pen the following words:

> Money is really needed,
> Money is really desired.
> Money rightfully mine,
> Come at the present time.

Write the amount of money you need on the paper (you do not *need* $1 million; remember, magick is practical and should be taken seriously). Put nine juniper berries and three sprigs of sage in the paper. Wrap with a gold ribbon. Place it on your altar. Repeat the chant for nine days at six hours after sunrise.

If you cannot perform the beginning of the spell at the given time, then cast the spell at night and repeat the chant six hours after sunrise thereafter.

SPEND PROPERLY

Prosperity is your divine right. Its abundance and ever-presence in your life is completely supported and encouraged by the Goddess and God. Your willingness to embrace prosperity is a spiritual manifestation of the wealth of heaven, equally available to all of us. This spell is designed to help you keep open the channel for affluence. It was created for those of you who have difficulty managing your money. When you get money, it burns a hole in your pocket. If you know it is coming, you spend it before it gets here and forget you owe your mom twenty bucks from the last time you spent your money too quickly. There never seems to be enough even though you work and know the money comes in. You haven't got the foggiest idea where it goes. You appear to be either swimming in dough or completely broke.

Obtain several pieces of any of the following: money draw or prosperity semiprecious stones for beading, such as green tourmaline, turquoise, tiger's eye, or citrine. Green tourmaline also represents the ability to transform negativity into positive situations. Turquoise is a master healer. Tiger's eye brings balance, while citrine is known as the merchant's stone. If you find one of these gems without a hole in the middle, you can wire wrap them instead. Light a green candle to represent money and an orange candle to symbolize divinity. You will call on Jupiter, who not only represents prosperity but the joy of living and business as well. Begin to chant the following:

THE TEEN SPELL BOOK

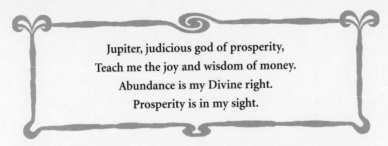
While chanting, place the stones in a vessel of water with a teaspoon of sea salt. After you take the stones out, waft money draw, prosperity, or Jupiter incense around them. Bead or wrap the stone into a necklace, bracelet, earrings, key chain, or whatever suits your creativity. Every once in a while, look into the flame of the candle, and when the creation is complete, repeat the chant.

Keep your prosperity amulet near or on you. This will not only help you draw prosperity, but it will keep it coming and help you spend it joyously as while as wisely.

PROBLEM-SOLVING
SPELLS

BANISH RUMORS

Kids at school can be nastier than the sleaziest of tabloids.
People make fun of things they do not understand. They feel
better by making light of their own ignorance and inabilities.
They might ridicule your good grades, your dark, reclusive
personality, or even your friendliness. Sometimes we can brush
off their hurtful words with humor, and other times rumors
work like a dentist's tool drilling into our nerves.

As much as you may want to return the favor and send some
nasty little rumors their way, I can promise you all that will do
is accrue your own negative karma. The Universe will take care
of the offender in time. Think about it: Anger is a learned
response. Those who ridicule and tease are often raised with
much criticism, scorn, or shame. They put others down so they
can fill the void in their own hearts, using you as a stepping
stone for all they lack. The fact is this is a temporary fix, as is
any high, and leaves them feeling hollow and hungry for more.
But you do not have to be their scapegoat any longer.

During a waning moon, grind one tablespoon of whole
cloves and two tablespoons of slippery elm leaves or bark with
a mortar and pestle, molcajete, or a big stone against a cutting
board. Be sure, however, that when you crush the cloves, it is
by hand and a grinding motion. The twisting and crushing is
symbolic of canceling out their negative words. As you grind,
chant

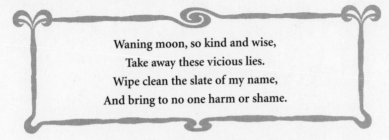

Waning moon, so kind and wise,
Take away these vicious lies.
Wipe clean the slate of my name,
And bring to no one harm or shame.

Put the resulting powder in an abalone shell, and take it to either a large body of water or a high place (a window in a tall apartment building or a mountaintop will work equally as well). Blow the powder into the wind, letting either the water or wind carry it away. Repeat the chant.

If they are in season, put snapdragons in a vase in your room as an extra device to ward others from talking trash about you.

BANISH SEXUAL HARASSMENT

Sexuality is power. Those who are weak and insecure attempt to steal others' power through many means, including sexual harassment. A bully attacks as a method of making him or herself feel better and filling that dark hole of self-loathing. People who sexually harass others are coming from a very weak and vulnerable position. They would have their victims believe that their femininity or masculinity and attractiveness are determined and valued by the offender's opinion, not their own.

On a piece of parchment paper, write the words *sexual harassment*. Around it write every word you can associate with the phrase—as if you were brainstorming. When you have exhausted every feeling you have on the subject, fold the paper and seal it with black wax (do this with a wax sealant kit or by dripping candle wax; just be careful not to burn yourself). At the top of the paper, draw an earth-banishing pentacle. You are releasing your attachment to the painful experience by realizing it is the offender who lacks the credibility to hurt others. You are also sending energy to counteract their offensive actions toward you. A pentacle is a physical representation of the pentagram, a five-pointed star in a circle, which symbolizes the four elements in balance with Spirit and is drawn like this:

Put the paper in the freezer and say

Your harassment now will freeze.

No longer will you provoke or tease.

Find the love in your heart

To leave me be as we part.

By My Will so Mote It Be!

When the harassment has stopped, bury the paper or burn it and safely discard the ashes.

BE INVITED

Our society cultivates a strong need to be social during the teen years. It is closely tied with the desire to feel you fit in and are accepted by others, aside from the fact that parties and dances are just plain fun! Whether you consider yourself a party animal or not, this spell can work for you.

Since Friday is the day of love, joy, and celebration, cast the spell on this day, preferably as soon as you hear about the event. Because this spell needs to manifest within a finite, fixed amount of time, you want to give the spell enough time to work. People get invited out because the host or date perceives they will add something wonderful to the atmosphere. These qualities might be humor, energy, popularity, or beauty.

Call on your favorite deity, the one who emulates the traits you admire most about yourself. Use the list on pages 30–45 if a god or goddess does not immediately come to mind. Girls, use either a cat- or female-shaped red or pink candle. Boys, use either a red or yellow male-shaped candle. Anoint the candle with your astrological oil as well as oil representing your favorite characteristics and/or the deity you have chosen to call on.

Place the candle in the south to represent life force and fun. Place anything that is representative of the event around the candle. Say

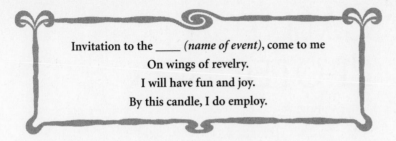

Invitation to the ____ *(name of event)*, come to me
On wings of revelry.
I will have fun and joy.
By this candle, I do employ.

Repeat the incantation for the next three days.

CALL FOR PROTECTION

Perhaps things have been tense at school or you are going to a concert at which you know will be a big, rowdy crowd. Maybe you are going white-water rafting or have a major sports event coming up. There are always times when we can use some extra protection.

The rune Algiz is the symbol for magickal protection. If you feel the need, you can wear a pendant with that rune drawn or inscribed on it to enhance protection. You can also use henna and tattoo the image of Algiz somewhere on your body. See page 58 for the Algiz image.

Carrying or wearing black tourmaline, obsidian, black onyx, or rainbow obsidian will also help keep you grounded, aware, and safe. Remember, these stones, symbols, and spells are not an excuse to take foolish risks. Always avoid being at the wrong place at the wrong time or with the wrong people. Be aware, and contact the warrior within. Do not make your guardian spirits work overtime.

To activate your Divine protection in times of need, follow this simple ritual. Concentrate on your second chakra, the area a couple of inches below your navel. Feel the energy building up in this area each time you take a breath. Repeat the following chant at least three times aloud or in your head:

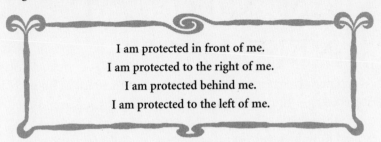

I am protected in front of me.
I am protected to the right of me.
I am protected behind me.
I am protected to the left of me.

As you repeat this, picture yourself surrounded by a golden circle of light that grows each time you say the phrase.

CAST OUT BAD ENERGY

When negative energy circulates through your room or house, it feels eerie—often cold and kind of hollow. If you were to get up in the middle of the night for a glass of water, you would be scared to walk down your own hallway. Or let's say you have a bad dream every night for a week, and the bad feelings seem to have taken form in the dark pockets throughout your house. Maybe you are in a great mood, and you notice after five minutes of resting on your bed, you start feeling cranky and irritable.

This ritual is called smudging. It was derived from a Native American tradition of purification and protection. You can either choose to buy sage bundles, readily available from metaphysical and magick shops, or make your own. Sage grows in desert climates, and in some areas is recovering from being an endangered plant, so take sparingly and only what you need. Never take more than one-third of the plant. Also be sure to leave an offering for Mother Earth, such as water, seeds, or a crystal. After you have collected about ten sage stems, bundle them together with yellow or red thread. Hang the sage upside-down in a dry, cool room for two to three days.

On the night of your ritual, burn frankincense incense in the center of the area you are blessing and protecting. Go outside to the farthest eastern corner of your property. (If you prefer to have more privacy, you can do this in your room.) Light the sage bundle, and blow out the flame until the leaves ember. Use a feather (a turkey feather works best) to direct the smoke away from you in a sweeping motion, and use an abalone shell or other fire-retardant container to catch the ashes. Decorate these tools by tying beads, special stones, or other talismans to the end of the feather or shell. Chant

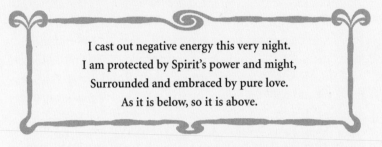

I cast out negative energy this very night.
I am protected by Spirit's power and might,
Surrounded and embraced by pure love.
As it is below, so it is above.

Move in a clockwise direction until you have blessed and protected all four corners, and then go into your house. Again, beginning in the east, direct the smoke to every high corner, around every window and door, and over every drain and toilet. When the smudging is complete, burn narcissus, lilac, or magnolia incense to bring in peace and harmony. This ritual will clear your house of all unwanted energy and prevent negativity from entering your home, while it seals in positive energy.

Get Rid of Nightmares

Most of us have had a bad dream. All dreams have messages for us. Our Higher Selves speak to us with familiar symbols and images to relay insight and warnings from the spiritual realm. Many books will help you interpret the symbol's meanings, and a few of my favorites are listed in the Resource Guide on page 263. I find it successful to confront the scary people and things in my dreams with courage, and just like an alter ego or bully with no real confidence of its own, the frightful image vanishes. I created and gave the image its power and am equally capable of taking it away.

But there comes a time when images, the sequence, or the message is so frightful and traumatic that it scares us beyond action. Some people are haunted by frightful reoccurring nightmares that make falling asleep a fearful experience. If this is the case for you, try this ritual. You can also do this for someone who you know is experiencing disturbing nightmares. Just think of them during the process, and if possible, look at a picture of them as well.

Obtain a kit for making a dreamcatcher, which is an ancient Native American tool used to weed out the bad dreams from the good. The web of the dreamcatcher literally traps the bad dreams, while the hole in the middle allows good dreams in.

Burn a white candle for protection during the project. Play children's lullabies or other soothing music to remind you of the protected innocence that is your true state. Anoint the pieces of the dreamcatcher with salted water to cast off former energies. As you make the dreamcatcher, chant

Bad dreams, bad dreams fade away.
You have lost your power this very day.
I call in loving dreams to help me *(or your friend's name)* sleep.
By protection of Spirit, this spell will keep.

Attach black tourmaline, tiger's eye, or mother of pearl to your creation somewhere. Follow Spirit's advice and direction; there is no wrong way to do this. Focus all of your intent into sending away the bad dreams and bringing in sweet, comforting dreams through the center. When the dreamcatcher is complete, pass the smoke of blessing incense around and through it.

Note: You may have unsuccessfully used a dreamcatcher to stop nightmares before. The difference here is that you made it, blessed it for a specific purpose, and adorned it with added power by the gems and other talismans that are sacred and powerful for you.

MAKE
CHORES
EASY

When many people first get into spellcasting, they think they will be able to cast a spell to turn their ex-girlfriend or ex-boyfriend into a toad or make a broom fly across the room. But then they find out magick is a way of life, an approach to living that puts them in touch with nature and their Higher Selves. Casting spells is a practice in adjusting thought patterns to bring about desires.

Wicca teaches us that the Universe exists outside ourselves, but that this life force also abides within. You can actually do nothing, physically or mentally, that could possibly add to what you already have. You have the capability to recognize that all your needs are already met, here in the present (pre-sent). Bringing about a change in awareness takes practice, so why not begin with an easy mantra to make everyday grunge work a little easier.

Each time you have a chore, whether it is dusting, vacuuming, taking out the trash, yard work, and so on, repeat this saying:

190

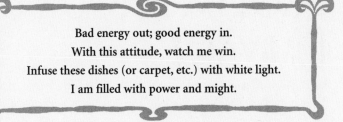

Bad energy out; good energy in.
With this attitude, watch me win.
Infuse these dishes (or carpet, etc.) with white light.
I am filled with power and might.

Protect Your Privacy

Setting boundaries for yourself is important for anyone of any age. We set boundaries to protect our bodies, our thoughts, and our space. Privacy is an important step in establishing the best we were meant to be. To keep others from encroaching on your private things, including your bedroom, try this spell.

Light a bundle of sage or separated sage leaves. Lightly blow on the herb until it embers. Pass the smoke over your whole body. Imagine roots sprouting from your feet, spreading throughout your entire room or space, and growing up the walls. This is the beginning of a magickal boundary that will make your personal space undesirable for others. Say

> Dear Goddess and God,
> Come to this ceremony
> As I set the boundaries
> To protect my privacy.

Call in protective animals, such as wolves, bears, or cougars—all of which are excellent for guarding territories—or your protectors may be angels, spirits of loved ones, or whatever makes you feel safe. Ask these guardians to stand post at the four directions for now and always. Beginning in the east, walk around your room in a clockwise direction, sprinkle sea salt, and call on each guide of the four corners. When you return to the east, thank your guides, the God, and the Goddess. Raise your hands in the air. Imagine yourself being filled with white light, and watch it fill all space until the room is full. Imagine the light moving out of the room to encircle the perimeter of your space with light. Your room is now sealed.

This spell is not to be cast so you can harm yourself or others within its boundaries.

RELEASE SOMEONE WHO HAS HARMED YOU

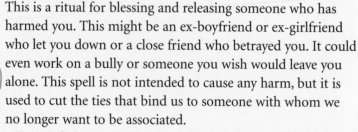

This is a ritual for blessing and releasing someone who has harmed you. This might be an ex-boyfriend or ex-girlfriend who let you down or a close friend who betrayed you. It could even work on a bully or someone you wish would leave you alone. This spell is not intended to cause any harm, but it is used to cut the ties that bind us to someone with whom we no longer want to be associated.

Sit quietly by yourself, and meditate for a few minutes to clear your mind. Just close your eyes and follow your breathing. When doing visualization work, you must be alone, relaxed, and somewhere private, like your room, your backyard, or patio. Doing this on the beach or at a park could work if it is not crowded, you know no one will disturb you, and it is a safe place to be. The idea is *no distractions*. If you are in your room, turn off your cell phone, pager, or computer.

When you are relaxed and peaceful, with your eyes closed, picture a blank movie screen in your head. The movie begins and you see the person you wish to release. You are now in the movie too, standing right in front of that person. Look them right in the eye, and with love in your heart, say this to them:

194

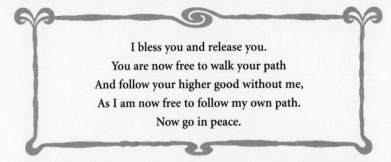

I bless you and release you.
You are now free to walk your path
And follow your higher good without me,
As I am now free to follow my own path.
Now go in peace.

Put your hands on the person's shoulders, turn them around, and watch them walk down a beautiful country road until you can no longer see them. You can open your eyes. You may find that if the attachment to the person is particularly strong, you have to repeat this process several times before it works. This is not a spell to do if you are temporarily mad at your mother or sister. Only do this if you are really serious about not having this person in your life anymore; it works.

SOLVE LEGAL MATTERS

There are many ways to run into trouble with the law. We all exist on energy vibrations, and if you have legal matters, a part of you attracted the world of legalities for you to learn a lesson regarding rules, stability, orderliness, faith, continuity, or possibly responsibility. Jupiter rules legal matters, and this god cannot imagine losing; he embodies the essence of faith, vitality, and confidence.

The intent of this spell is to sway judicial decisions in your favor. If you have committed a crime, you will not be relieved of your responsibility to repay your karma, with this spell or any other. But you can hope to achieve a lighter sentence by your admittance of wrongdoing and willingness to settle up with the Universe. Your compliance and readiness shows courage, and that will be rewarded. If you have found yourself in a legal battle, such as a car accident that was not your fault or being a victim of a crime, have faith in Jupiter and stand firm in your innocence.

Cast this spell on a Thursday. Light two brown candles for grounding, and anoint them with Jupiter oil. Place them on either side of a white image candle that has been anointed with your astrological oil. Grind two tablespoons of rue (the name of this herb originates from the Greek word *reuo,* which means "set free"), the petals from three marigolds, and three sprigs of chamomile with a mortar and pestle. While you grind, say

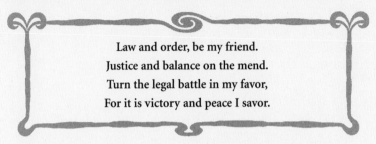

Law and order, be my friend.
Justice and balance on the mend.
Turn the legal battle in my favor,
For it is victory and peace I savor.

Sprinkle the herbs in a purple cloth, and tie with a gold ribbon. Repeat the incantation. Take the pouch with you to court.

SCHOOL AND WORK
SPELLS

GET ON THE TEAM

Team playing teaches us how to rely on others. Through sports and other organizations that foster camaraderie, we learn the value of having the support of others, the strength of combined efforts, and how to share. We discover that sacrificing self-centered needs benefits the good of the team. This might be demonstrated by curtailing weekend nighttime activities for optimum performance at games, putting energy and time into practice, or selling everything from Christmas wreaths to wrapping paper to pay for your team to go to Hawaii. The higher you go in sports, the more this is true.

On the other hand, team playing also fosters competitiveness. This challenges you to improve on your performance. Your ego is rewarded when you apply practice and focus. The workout itself becomes the payoff. Confidence and self-esteem grow while you enjoy healthy physical expression.

Lastly, getting on the team satisfies a basic human desire: to feel you belong. It seems as if the longing for community was programmed into us. Most people are not completely self-sufficient and do rely on others for survival. Some have a talent for farming while others know smithcrafting. Long ago societies began trading the products from these abilities, and the need for cooperation was born.

Cast this spell on a Tuesday night, because Mars, the Roman god of war, courage, assertiveness, and athleticism, rules this day. You will also invoke Apollo, a Greek and Roman god, to represent strength. Inscribe a red image candle (if you are a girl, use a feminine form; if you are a boy, use a male form) with your astrological sign and an image of the team you want to join. Anoint the candle with Apollo or Mars oil as well as your astrological oil. Place two yellow candles to represent your will on either side of the image candle. Anoint them with the Apollo or Mars oil as well. Burn dragon's blood incense for power and might.

Place a symbol of the team (such as a baseball, chess piece, or pom-pom) on the altar but far away from the flame of the candles. Hold your hands with your palms toward the altar. Take three deep breaths, and imagine yourself being chosen for the team. Say

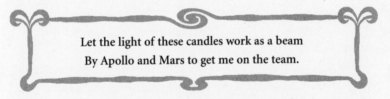

Let the light of these candles work as a beam
By Apollo and Mars to get me on the team.

You can also choose to visualize the position you want to play, but this can be limiting, as the coach may have in mind an even more suitable position for your skills.

GET IN THE SAME CLASS AS YOUR FRIENDS

No doubt about it, having a friend in class makes it easier to get through the most boring teacher or subject. We have all been stuck in a class in which the clock seems to move slower than molasses in winter, and no one we know surrounds us. Sometimes this forces us into learning something we never would have paid attention to before, which is a good lesson in and of itself, but this spell is about fun.

There is nothing the matter with combining fun and learning. Teachers who embrace this attitude often have more students excelling than not. Whether it is a matter of humor, putting lessons to music, or just lighting up the atmosphere of the room, fun can enhance learning.

Cast this spell at the end of summer or winter break at least two weeks before school starts. Concentrate on the people you would like to have in class as well as the attitude of the teacher and atmosphere of the room. Some teachers are such sticklers that even if you had ten of your best buds in class, they would not so much as let you look sideways at them without an embarrassing or offending punishment. So keep your focus on the feeling you desire, not just the right combination of people.

202

Get two different colors of modeling clay: your favorite color and either a color that represents a particular friend or pink to represent any friend. Fashion the clay into people. Form one person in your favorite color to resemble you and the other to symbolize your friend. Get a picture or statue of the Tibetan goddess Tara, and place your play dough images on either side of her. Say

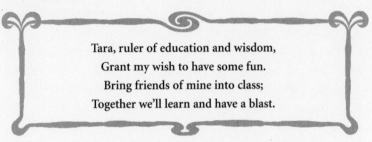

> Tara, ruler of education and wisdom,
> Grant my wish to have some fun.
> Bring friends of mine into class;
> Together we'll learn and have a blast.

Leave the images in place until the first day of school.

HAVE A GOOD FIRST DAY OF SCHOOL

Everyone wants to make a good impression on the first day of school. One of the most important aspects of being happy there or anywhere is attitude. If you wake up and say to yourself, "This is a bad day" or "I hate Monday," and so on, then no amount of spellwork will help you. What is inside yourself really makes your day. You color every event in your life by your outlook and the way you approach it. Your attitude determines whether or not you will make a good impression.

Know that every day is in harmony with the Divine order. Harmony begins as an idea or thought, eventually manifesting in your actions and character. Perform this ritual the night before school starts, and play classical or other soothing music. Place one teaspoon of valerian root and one teaspoon of lavender in a piece of blue or purple cloth six inches square. Repeat the word: "Harmony." Concentrate on the images of harmony as you chant the word: "Harmony, harmony, harmony." What do you see? The scenes that flash through your mind will bring you under the law of harmony, which blesses and protects not only you, but everyone in your experience every day. Sprinkle two drops of orange blossom oil, and continue chanting. Fold the cloth over the herbs, and secure the fabric with a silver ribbon. Say this affirmation:

All ideas that are needed for today are complete in mind
And communicate themselves to meet each human need.
There are not many minds—only one—
And this one does the guiding and the guarding.

This is scientific fact, and you can go no higher. The next morning when you wake, smile. Focus on an object or music if that is what you wake up to.

Think about any positive aspects you will look forward to for the day. Rise from bed, light a candle, and meditate as you continue to wake up. Say to yourself, "Good things will happen, because I am looking forward to the day!" Also add such statements as, "I look great today" or "I get to see my friends all day." Say these to yourself several times as the candle burns. As you shower and get dressed, continue to say them. Put out the candle, and remember the flame as it warms your day. Carry the pouch with you on your first day of school. And have a good one!

LAND THE JOB

Throughout our lives most of us will have jobs. Jobs give us purpose and make us feel productive. From our efforts, we earn money or other valuable trading items. One of the most important gifts a job offers, though, is a sense of independence. Finally, we are cultivating something that we alone created. We can contribute to the household needs, buy magickal tools, or go out with friends. A job opens up a world of opportunities.

You need to put your best foot forward when applying for the job of your desire. Be sure to dress appropriately, speak articulately, and follow through with your application and/or interview. These are all things that can be done on the physical level and need to be done to give this spell its power.

Cast the spell during the waxing of the moon, preferably on a Thursday. You will need three colored candles: green for opportunity, yellow to bring in your desire successfully, and red for action (because you probably needed the job yesterday and would like this spell to work as quickly as possible). Burn money draw incense (available at most Wiccan stores or see Resource Guide, page 263). You will anoint each candle with job or pine oil. As you rub the oil on your candles, chant

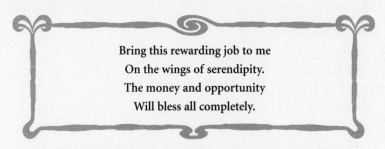

Bring this rewarding job to me
On the wings of serendipity.
The money and opportunity
Will bless all completely.

Light the candles and repeat the chant three times. Allow the flame to burn for at least ten minutes before dousing with a candle snuffer.

LESSEN HOMEWORK

We can combat the issue of an overload of homework in two ways. First, you will work on the mind of the teacher to ease up on the assignments, and second, you will concentrate on changing your attitudes toward the homework itself.

People say teachers have communicated a message well when the student can explain it back. That is why you often have to show your work for math problems or submit rough drafts of a paper. The first part of the spell is about convincing teachers you know what they are saying and that three hours of homework may not help you understand any better. But the first part of the spell is only a presentation of allowing teachers to look at the homework load differently. If it is not in their will to change their minds, there is nothing you can or should do to cast a spell over them.

Second, we will focus on your attitude. If you are angry and resist working on your homework, you are going to have to battle that before you get started. Every battle takes energy. This energy will be better directed on seeing the homework as a necessary hurdle.

Do this ritual whenever you feel overloaded with your homework. Stack your homework, books, and notes in the easternmost quadrant of your studying space. This direction rules all mental activity. Add a dash of salt and two drops of moon or lotus oil to a cup of water. Both these scents help subtle changes. Lightly sprinkle a wand with the water. You can even designate a tree branch as your wand, just make sure to consecrate it first. See page 48 for directions. Wave the wand over the stack and say

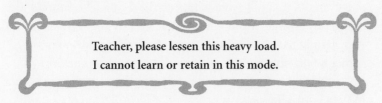

Teacher, please lessen this heavy load.
I cannot learn or retain in this mode.

Add two drops of rosemary or sandalwood oil, for mental powers, to the water. Lightly sprinkle your wand with the water. Wave it over the stack and say

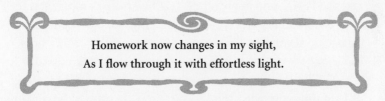

Homework now changes in my sight,
As I flow through it with effortless light.

Burn rosemary incense while you study and do your homework. This will keep you alert and focused on the task at hand. Also place at your desk a clear quartz crystal that has been soaked in salt water and has lain under the light of the full moon. This stone facilitates mental clarity and allows for changes in perception.

Make Colleges Beg for You

Not all of us can score 1500 on the SATs, have the athletic ability to attain a full scholarship, or the financial resources to afford any college of our choosing. It may be that no one in your family has gone to college, so you lack support and someone driving you to continue when your own determination has failed. The first thing is to try to do everything possible to help yourself along.

As you probably know, it is in the junior year of high school that most colleges look at scholarship candidates, so really try to keep your grades up. Learn one new vocabulary word each week, take the PSATs, and apply for every scholarship you can. You may even choose to begin your higher learning at a community college until you can earn money for a bigger four-year school. But shoot for the moon before you settle on the nearest star.

You will assemble an altar in the eastern direction—symbolic of beginnings, intellect, and inspiration—to attract those prime schools. Gather as much as you can that represents your favorite colleges (that is, sweatshirts, postcards, pennants, mugs, and so on). If you get a chance to visit the campus, bring back something from the surrounding nature, such as a leaf, a fistful of dirt, snow, or sand, or a to-go menu, napkin, or coaster from your likely hangout.

Place a picture of Janus, the two-faced Roman god on your altar. If you have difficulty finding his image, draw a picture of him, or write down his qualities on a piece of parchment paper: possibilities, new endeavors, the turn of the year, overcoming obstacles, and opportunity. Burn a sage bundle for wisdom to make the right choices. Light a yellow candle for mental clarity. Hold a piece of turquoise in your dominant hand and say

> I call to me the college of my choice
> To improve my mind and strengthen my voice.
> Here I will learn all I need to know,
> As I learn, all sides of me will grow.

Lay the stone next to the collegiate items.

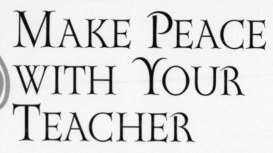

MAKE PEACE WITH YOUR TEACHER

The world is a mirror, and there is only one source. Consider this source to be the sun, and every creation on earth is a ray of light from that sun. We are all connected and need one another to be brilliant and whole. When others are upset with you, they often see something in you, a personality or physical trait, which they wish they had or one they have and wish they did not.

There are times when we are going to run into people who do not like us—it is inevitable. Sometimes we can just remove ourselves from the situation, and other times it is a situation that needs to be experienced by both parties.

Try using a pendulum to assess whether this is a manhole you can walk away from or a hurdle you must jump over. Ask if you can leave the class and the teacher. If the pendulum goes back and forth in a straight line, the answer is no. If it moves in circles, ask for a transfer. Test the pendulum by asking if you need to stay. If it circles yes, then proceed with this spell.

Cast the spell on a Wednesday (the day that rules communication), and if you can help it, do not do this during a Mercury Retrograde (check astrological charts, call metaphysical stores,

212

or review the Web sites listed in the back of this book). Mercury Retrograde confuses communication and often causes interaction spells to backfire. Also, by the Wiccan Rede, you should never cast a spell over someone. This spell should be cast with an intent of infusing peace, harmony, and communication between you and your teacher.

You will be invoking Brigid, the Irish goddess. Burn a purple candle for intuition and Divine law. Remember a particularly bad incident with your teacher. On a piece of parchment paper, draw symbols that relate to the incident or write out the whole scenario. Wrap an amethyst, the stone of healing, peace, communication, and anger management, in the paper. Seal it with wax from the candle, being careful not to burn yourself. As you do this ritual, chant

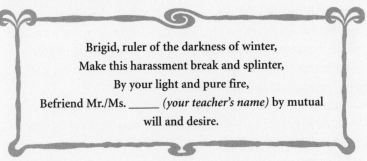

Brigid, ruler of the darkness of winter,
Make this harassment break and splinter,
By your light and pure fire,
Befriend Mr./Ms. _____ *(your teacher's name)* by mutual will and desire.

Bury the pouch in your yard.

PASS THE CLASS

There is a difference between wanting to know the answers to a test and just plain getting an *A* in a class. You can definitely have both, but before you cast this spell, figure out your motivation. What exactly is it that you want? In the many different subjects and arenas of life, some of us are learners and some of us are students. Depending on the area of interest, some people want to absorb the information and be able to apply it to further learning, possibly related to a career, and others just want a good grade—their focus is elsewhere. If you want to be an architect, then physics may hold more interest and be more important than it might be to a would-be professional writer. Keep your focus in mind.

There is only one mind, one source that is omniscient (all knowing). There are no new ideas under the sun, because they all derive from the same source. You and your teacher receive intelligence from the same limitless mind. Connect back to Spirit's home, and you will find the answers.

Gather fresh lavender or rosemary leaves (dried will do as well but are not as powerful). Both of these herbs stimulate memory. Put the herbs in a purple pouch. This color relates to intelligence and higher learning. Say

> There is only one source of intelligence.
> During the test I will be open, not tense.
> The answers will come effortlessly.
> I call forth the highest grade for me.

Then you are actually going to have to crack open the book or your notes. While you study, breathe in your herb-scented pouch. Take the pouch with you to class for the test. Calm and center your mind before you begin. Repeating the above chant will also help. You can also use your pouch when you have a block while writing papers and other forms of difficulty with homework.

I used this for business law in my junior year. I needed an *A*, just 90 percent on the final, to bring up my grade and GPA for possible colleges. I not only got the grade I had in mind, but I got a 91 percent! To me this was an affirmation of the Divine at work.

WIN THE
ELECTION

You've made the posters—got up at 6:00 A.M. to plaster them all over the school. The speech is written, and soon you'll stand up in front of between fifty and five hundred people and talk for five long minutes. Then there will be the wait, the call slip to excuse you from class to sit in a room with the other nervous candidates. Part of you will remain as cool as ice. That will be your poker face. But inside you may be as frantic as a turkey the day before Thanksgiving.

First of all, you must congratulate yourself on coming this far. It takes a lot of guts to voice your desires. There may be little more you want right now than to win the election. It is that focus and ambition you need to put into this spell.

This spell will work best if performed during the waxing of the moon and on a Wednesday. Wednesday is ruled by Mercury, the planet of communication; hence your popularity will be greatly affected by its influence. You are going to create a white image candle. An image candle represents you. Anoint the candle with your astrological oil. Inscribe the candle with any symbols you feel represent you, such as your zodiac sign, your favorite or power animal, or your magickal name. In this ritual you will call on Dionysus, a Greek god who, among many things, represents fun, festivities, vegetation, and wine. He holds androgynous energy, so males and females can invoke him equally. Surround the white image candle with two yellow candles for communication and courage, two orange candles to represent Dionysus and cheerfulness, and a green candle for Dionysus and abundance. Anoint all the candles with grape oil, and say

> I call upon Dionysus to aid me tonight.
> Help me win the election in my sight.
> Bring the majority votes in my favor.
> With your help, a victory I will savor.

Begin lighting the perimeter candles, and repeat the chant for each lighting. Lastly, light the white candle. Reflect on all the good you will do while in office. Allow the candle to burn for ten minutes. Douse the flames with a candle snuffer.

SELF-IMPROVEMENT
SPELLS

ACCEPT YOUR BODY

Sometimes we pray for obstacles to be removed before determining why they are in our lives. Like a diamond, however, if we did not have little nicks, many unique facets, and "imperfections," our light would not be as brilliant. A diamond in the rough is dull and plain, but one that has a unique blend of incisions, like the many features of our body and personality, is beautiful and unique. As stated by Martha Graham in *Dance to the Piper* (Boston: Little, Brown, 1951), "Because there is only one you in all of time, this expression is unique. And if you block it, it will never exist through any other medium and be lost. The world will not have it. It is not your business to determine how good it is nor how valuable nor how it compares with other expressions. It is your business to keep it yours clearly and directly."

Early in the morning, before the dew has evaporated from the grass and flowers, take the petals from one fresh rose (preferably pink or red). Light a pink candle. You may choose to cast a circle or set a sacred space by imagining you are one with all the goodness of the Universe. Fill an ice cube tray with fresh springwater, and place one petal in each cube space. Place the tray in the freezer. As you do this, reflect on Martha Graham's words. See yourself as a diamond that needs a bit of polishing so you can shine from each facet of your unique being. When the water has turned to ice, place the cubes in a glass of pink lemonade. Reflect on turning your bitterness (like lemon juice) about your body to sweet love (like the rose petals). Drink this beverage every day for one week at your favorite time of day. Soon you will learn to honor everything about yourself that makes you a blessing to the rest of us.

ATTAIN A PERFECT COMPLEXION

Okay, you've got a zit the size of Mount Everest on your nose. Before you cast this spell, ask yourself if you have done everything on the mundane level to get rid of the little beast. Still not working? Well, there is not much to say about this spell, but get it done and get it done fast.

Although pimples pop up all throughout the year and through every phase of the moon cycle, if you can wait, cast this spell during a waning moon or on a Saturday—at least repeat it during the fading of the moon.

Some say there are metaphysical reasons for every physical ailment: what appears on the body first shows up in the mind. According to Louise Hay's book *You Can Heal Your Life,* a possible reason for acne may include small outbursts of anger, resentment toward self, or the expression of repressed feelings. Obviously, the skin of a teenager lends itself to producing the nasty protrusions. But consider the idea and whether or not it applies to you. If pimples seem to just appear at times you don't like yourself, are stressed out, or are mad, pay close attention to accepting yourself and life just the way you and it are.

So, while the moon is getting smaller, cut an apple across the middle. The seeds form the five-pointed star known as the pentacle. The pentacle is a symbol of the four elements, known

THE TEEN SPELL BOOK

as air, fire, water, and earth, in balance with Spirit. Rub the apple over the affected area. Say

> Apple, sacred fruit of the Goddess,
> With this gift, I do caress
> The pimple that brought me shame.
> I banish this zit in your name.

Slice another apple from top to bottom. The seeds form the shape of a heart (however irregular). Rub this apple over your acne as well. Say

> I love and accept myself as I am today.
> Clear skin I summon to come my way.
> By My Will so Mote It Be
> Three times three times three.

Bury the first apple by a tree, bush, or flower—preferably outside and not in a potted plant. It doesn't have to be on your own property. This will allow the nature spirit to carry the energy of the acne away. Bury the second apple by water or where water gathers. If you can't find such a place, just pour clean water over your burial. This symbolizes allowing the element of water to wash your face clean.

BE BRAVE

Building your courage begins with little steps. You can use this spell for a variety of reasons, from standing up to peer pressure or someone who hurts or intimidates you to phobias such as a fear of heights or closed-in spaces.

To rid ourselves of fear, we must confront whatever scares us. Fear carries with it a sporadic vibration and grows when we feed it energy. In actuality, fear is really an acronym for *false evidence appearing real*. The only way a fear is going to leave is to meet it head-on. To accomplish this, you must arm yourself as if you were going into battle. Bravery is required for any battle. With bravery and courage comes strength of heart, a strong conviction of your rights and confidence. Courage comes under the realm of Mars, the Roman god of war.

To give this spell its greatest potency, work on one fear at a time, and be sure it is necessary to release it for your overall good. Cast the spell on Tuesday, as Mars rules that day. Because Mars is known as the Red Planet, anything you can do to bring this color into the incantation would be helpful. Obtain a stone of bloodstone, garnet, or ruby; it can be a stand-alone stone or jewelry, just as long as it is yours. Light a red candle. Anoint the stone with either cypress or rose geranium oil. Rub the oil into the stone, and imagine yourself doing whatever it is you fear. It is not necessary to imagine yourself going above and beyond reasonable expectations. What you need to seek is balance. For example, if you want to stand up to a bully, do not visualize

224

the bully in turn being afraid of you. That does not serve anyone's highest good. Just imagine the situation being resolved. As you rub in the oil, chant

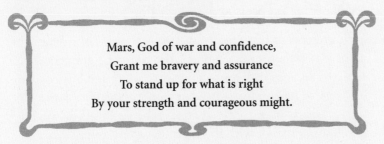

Mars, God of war and confidence,
Grant me bravery and assurance
To stand up for what is right
By your strength and courageous might.

It is best to begin with little steps toward bravery to build your confidence and self-esteem. You do not have to swim across the lake, around the pier, or competitively to overcome your fear of water. Carry the stone with you until you have successfully faced your fear. Afterward place it on your altar as a reminder of your courage and the obstacles you are willing to face.

BEFRIEND YOUR WEAKNESSES

Spirit presents us with disadvantages as a means of strengthening us. Often these "weak points" turn out to be our greatest strengths because they protect our core selves and offer us the discovery of new abilities that can empower us. The dark, unseen aspects of ourselves are not going away, so you might as well make friends with them. As the saying goes: Keep your friends close but your enemies closer.

By making friends with our weaknesses, we can turn them into our guardians. If you ignore weaknesses, they can take over, or worse, you may project them onto others, attributing your downfalls to other people. In other words, you will see others as the ones who are flaky, insecure, or too loud, when in reality, it is you.

On a sunny day, during the time of the waning moon, light a brown candle for being centered in the truth and a yellow candle for the courage to come face to face with the things you like least about yourself. You can do this either outside or in a sheet of sunlight streaming through a room. Play your favorite music. Place corresponding elements at each direction, such as a feather in the east, an orange candle in the south, a cup filled with water in the west, and a pentagram in the north. Slowly spin in a circle three times in a clockwise direction. You may

THE TEEN SPELL BOOK

even choose to dance a bit. With each turn, visualize a white light filling your body with positive energy.

When you dance under the warmth and comfort of the sun, there will always be a shadow. It is similar to the reflection found in a mirror—it is an aspect of the truth, but it is in reverse. Watch your shadow play against the walls or trees. Imagine you are dancing with each part of your personality that you dislike, and make friends with each part. Notice how your rhythm is affected each time you move into a new emotion. Send yourself love each time a pang of hurt arises for being the way you were made. You are perfect just the way you are and a gift to everyone who knows you.

Light is always stronger than darkness, and that silver lining can take over an entire gray, billowing cloud—if only you will believe it can.

DEAL WITH SHYNESS

Shyness is common to most everyone in some form or another. One of my best friends is terribly shy but deals with it in an extraordinary way. When she feels particularly unsure of herself, she actually gets loud and boisterous. It is a distraction and avoidance from the real concern, which she readily admits. Others combat this anxiety with jokes or by withdrawing. A commonly held misconception about shy people is that they are stuck-up, shallow, or even obnoxious. In life we often swing the pendulum to mask our darkest concerns and dislikes about ourselves. One way to overcome this shyness is to become part of a group or club that interests you or by merely talking to your locker neighbor. It's kind of a "Fake it 'til you make it" idea.

Cast this spell during the waxing of the moon. Sit in front of a white, unlit candle, and take three deep connected breaths. Imagine yourself as a confident mighty oak tree that is completely stable, powerful, and calm. Once relaxed, light the candle and visualize the flame opening up your heart chakra. Envision your heart opening as a pink rose unfolding its petals. See the brilliant color spilling out into the world. Picture a flood of pink light flowing from your heart and mingling with the white energy from the candle. Visualize the white candle as another person or group of people, your energy mixing with

228

theirs in conversation, laughter, and partying. You are separate yet together.

Repeat this affirmation:

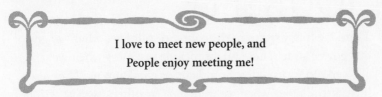

I love to meet new people, and
People enjoy meeting me!

Repeat this affirmation as many times as you feel necessary. Practice speaking to the candle as if you are meeting someone for the first time. Start a conversation based on a class or someone's name, complement them on their clothes or style of writing, or whatever. Finish your conversation and say, "See you later," to the candle, while putting out the flame. Repeat this spell as often as you wish, and it will become second nature for you to begin a conversation with anyone!

(This spell comes to us from Myrddann, a Wiccan High Priest and Ordained Minister of the Progressive Universal Life Church.)

EMPOWER YOURSELF

There are many times in the course of our lives when we give our power away. These might include instances when we allowed others to judge, humiliate, or condemn us. They also include the times when we were hurt by others' words, action, and inaction. Instead of living in the present moment, we allow these little hurts to build into mountains of pain.

Guided by the woman who donated this process for the book, when I did this exercise I went back to a lifetime from the thirteenth century (see her information at the end of the ritual). Now, you don't have to believe in reincarnation to be Wiccan or understand this process.

I saw myself at four years old dressed in a beautiful gown with long braids and ribbons flowing down my back standing outside our castle. I was saying good-bye to my father who was leaving us. When I asked him why he wouldn't stay, he replied that he couldn't stand up to my mother. Regardless of what this meant to me, he needed to feel he was a man—elsewhere. It was implied he would come back for me. From this point forward I based my perceptions of men and how I could win their love upon this scene.

Many symbols and relationships within the vision parallel the life I have experienced this time around. It is as if I am reliving

230

a similar experience but have been given the choice and understanding that it is possible to respond differently. The person I imagined for the visualization was not my father but my four-year-old self.

My sister just completed this process as well. In her experience, which she described as transformational, amazing, and unbelievable, she felt her entire body tingle, it was as if her legs were on fire, her head spinning, and her arms lay limp and heavy as she traversed time to discover a moment when she gave her power away.

The beauty of this work is the freedom it gives you. No one can take away your power without your permission. One incident can color and inhibit similar relationships for eons of time. But once you shed light and understanding and gain true perspective, you can live more fully, with power and grace.

You will be focusing on your solar plexus—the conductor and center of self-worth, confidence, self-esteem, choice, and power for this ritual. At some point during the visualization you may feel intense distractions, the need to run away or stop the process. But keep going, these are just your ego's little diversions to sidetrack you from releasing the pain and connecting yourself to Spirit.

You may want to tape this process. Begin by taking three deep breaths. Inhale through the nose and exhale through the mouth. Breathe another three deep breaths. Inhale through the mouth and exhale through the nose.

See, sense, or feel the person, symbol, or situation with which you have an issue or problem. Personify (give a face and body to) the symbol or situation. Imagine them or it standing or sitting in front of you. Look directly in his or her eyes or at the symbol. See the area above their solar plexus and watch it open. See or feel this area open in your own body.

See, sense, or feel energy, all the power *you* gave them or it, coming from his, her, or its solar plexus back to your solar plexus. If you need or want to, you can demand your power back with words. Pull all your strength back into your body. If it helps, you can also choose to see you and the person or symbol in the place where the pain originated. Continuing visualizing this stream of energy until you no longer feel the need to or the stream disappears. You have a right to take all your power back.

See, sense, or feel a stream of energy going from your solar plexus to their or its solar plexus. You are handing back all the baggage you have carried around for them. In this process you can also give them a gift, such as a flower, candle, or seashell. They have offered you the chance to learn a lesson, and the present can be symbolic of ending this cycle. Continue this visualization until there is no energy left to give back.

See, sense, or feel your solar plexus area, and that of the other person or symbol filled with white light. See the "karmic cord" between the two of you dissolve and completely disappear. See your solar plexus area and that of the other close shut.

Allow yourself to talk to them or it. Say all the things you have ever said or wanted to say. Get *everything* off your chest;

literally free your heart center of all burdens. Now allow yourself to listen with your soul-self when they or it talk(s) to you. This will feel like you are listening from your heart center, or at your third eye (the space between your eyebrows) or you may even hear their words from a space around your body. Be open to whatever words come through. Let the person or symbol get everything off their or its chest. Allow yourself to be a channel and do not force the words or assume you know what they/it might say.

Now allow yourself to hug or touch the person or symbol in the most loving, healthy way possible. Look at their/its face. Has it changed?

See, sense, or feel the person or symbol walking or fading away until they or it disappear(s). Take three deep breaths. Inhale through the nose and exhale through the mouth. Breathe another three deep breaths.

This process will begin to free you from the associations to the pain attached to the person or symbol. It does not dictate that they or it will not be in your life. It simply gives your power back, so you can make a conscious decision when you encounter the person, symbol, or situation again to be strong regardless of their presence or absence.

Nila F. Keith, C.H.T. who has been in private practice for fifteen years, gave this process to us. She specializes in in-depth guidance of calling back your power and retrieving your fragmented soul parts. You can contact Nila at wakan@pacbell.net.

EXCEL AT YOUR HOBBY

We will entertain many hobbies over the course of a lifetime. The most important factor that will change a hobby into a serious pursuit is your attention. Whatever you give your full attention to will transition from a pastime that only receives half of your attention to a career or long-lasting goal. So the first step of this spell is focusing on the aspect of your hobby in which you want to excel. Be specific; for example, if you are on the debate team, decide whether you want to improve on your delivery, rebuttal, or initial presentation. An overall improvement with this spell is possible, but as always, the ritual will have more punch with a clearer channel and more focused intent.

If you are involved in many things, from sports to chess to needlepoint, narrow your attention to that which appeals to you the most. One way to determine this is to gather one rock for each activity. Write one hobby on each rock. Turn the rocks over, and take three deep breaths. Center yourself by imaging a white light starting in your solar plexus (the space between your upper ribcage) and descending to the depths of the earth. When you are ready, circle your hand three times counterclockwise (widdershins) over the rocks and say

> Take away the hobby of least desire.
> Bring to me that which calls me higher.
> I pull the rock to be released
> And with it, all anxiety is ceased.

Do this until you have only one rock left. Place the chosen rock on your altar. With your third eye (also known as your mind's eye or sixth chakra), see yourself reaching the pinnacle of achievement in this hobby, which is now dubbed a serious pursuit. Circle your hand three times clockwise (deosil) around the rock. Say

> I bring to me success and victory
> Within the realm of history.
> Through _____ (your desire) and hard work employed,
> I shall excel, good times enjoyed.
> By My Will so Mote It Be,
> Three times three times three.

FIND GRACE AND STYLE

A lot of growing up occurs in the teen years, both physically and emotionally. And with these growth spurts come growing pains. If you have transitioned from a tomboy into the world of girls or are just dealing with six inches of growth during the span of one summer and you have no idea where your limbs end, this spell is for you.

Grace is typically an attribute associated with female energy and the Goddess. As you cast this spell, wear dark blue and use as much of the color as you can with candles and stones—especially lapis lazuli, flowers (even some lavender), and so on. Goddess energy resonates to the power of blue, which calls forth nurturing, balancing vibrations. Notice, too, that blue is the color of the throat chakra, and the swan is well known for its graceful neckline. You will mainly concentrate on the purity and elegance of the swan, the archetypical animal of grace and style that is particularly sacred to Aphrodite, Venus, and Sarasvati.

Arrange your blue sacred objects in a semicircle around a picture of a swan. Light a blue candle. Hold the lapis in your hand. Close your eyes and visualize yourself surrounded by gray mist. You are a swan—beautiful and graceful, gliding across a woodland pool. The sky turns from indigo to a pale

THE TEEN SPELL BOOK

blue. The last star disappears as the sun kisses the horizon. With the sun's first light pink, orange, and yellow colors dash across the sky. The morning mist turns into a silvery veil that lifts all around you as it ascends toward heaven. You continue to glide effortlessly and poised with grace and style. Chant

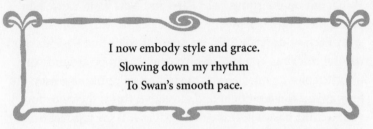

I now embody style and grace.
Slowing down my rhythm
To Swan's smooth pace.

Open your eyes and watch the candlelight. Repeat the chant nine times over the next three days. Carry the stone with you until you feel swan's energy and medicine descend upon you.

GET THE BEST WARDROBE

Watch out on the runways of Paris and New York, 'cause here you come! Getting a sweet wardrobe begins with color and style. Each of us has a hue and range of color that best fits our natural coloring. You can revolve your wardrobe around your favorite color or maybe even the hottest color of the season. As long as you feel confident and attractive, this is the color for you. Get the basics in this color, such as a T-shirt, jacket or sweater, skirt (of the season's or your favorite length), pants, shorts, and a swimsuit.

Next ask yourself about your style. Do you like department stores, vintage or thrift shops, or boutiques? Is there a time period, like the '40s, '60s or '80s, that really calls to you?

For this incantation, you will need to collect catalogs from your favorite stores, a variety of magazines, glue or paste, and a sketchpad. On a Friday, which is special to style because Venus rules this day and abides over art and beauty, cut out your favorite styles, colors, and looks you would like to see in your closet and on your body. Do not look at the price or wonder where you would wear it or if you have the courage.

You are going to glue the pictures in your sketchpad, or draw your desired clothes using color pencils. You can choose to arrange the photos or pictures by theme (color, season, dressy, casual, etc.) or in an eclectic style. It depends on your fashion attitude. Do you switch easily between grunge wear and teatime with Grandma, or do you change style from one event to the next at all? Play your favorite music. You can choose to do this with a friend, as long as there is no judgment whatsoever cast by either of you.

When the book is complete (or near completion—you may choose to have this be a work in progress), anoint it with two drops of rose oil. Place four small clear quartz crystals on the corners of your book. Cup your hands over the closed book or on a special page. Keep your fingers sealed close together. Breathe three times deeply. Imagine a brilliant rainbow. The sun catches the light perfectly and draws a picture-perfect kaleidoscope of color. Pull that rainbow toward your heart center. See the light travel through your body and out your hands, infusing the book with color and energy. Direct the energy for at least one minute before releasing, and then leave your book on your altar. Surround the book with flowers, such as dahlia (for physical beauty), jasmine (for elegance), roses (for beauty), or sunflowers (for radiance).

Learn How to Trust Again

When I was fourteen, I had a best friend I truly adored. One day we got into a fight, and she went back to her previous best friend. Once we were all in the locker room getting ready for P.E. when the two girls wrapped their arms around each other and sang an old song: "Reunited and it feels so good. . . ." Their tone was mocking as they sneered at me. I tried to ignore them as I tied my shoes, but of course, it didn't work. For a long time, I was haunted by their sarcastic singing, causing me to shy away from anyone who might call me their best friend. By keeping my own feelings protected, I would not have to feel the pain of losing a friend again. But these walls also serve to keep us from knowing true companionship and friendship.

Cast this spell on a Saturday for banishment. Gather the rose petals from one pink or red rose, two sprigs of rosemary, and one teaspoon of witch hazel. Write with dove's blood ink or a silver pen on a piece of parchment paper the following words:

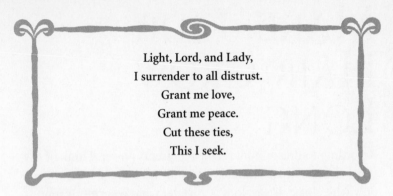

Light, Lord, and Lady,
I surrender to all distrust.
Grant me love,
Grant me peace.
Cut these ties,
This I seek.

Wrap your gatherings in the parchment paper. Burn the paper in a safe container such as a fireplace, fire pit, or sizable cauldron. Repeat the chant nine times over the next three days.

MAKE YOUR HAIR GROW LONG

According to dream books, hair represents power. Think of the story of Samson and Delilah. Samson was invincibly strong only when his hair was long. Consider what your motivation is to have long hair. Is it to feel powerful or beautiful, or is it something else? Keep this focus in mind; if your intent is clear, the result of your spell will be more satisfying.

Also, this is definitely a case in which you need to be sure you have done everything on the physical level to manifest your wish before you bother casting the spell. Have you conditioned your hair regularly, brushed it every night consecutively for weeks on end without result, or are you dying it three colors every other week? Another method for stronger hair is to pull a pick through it after conditioning while still in the shower. This way you will not cause as many split ends or need to brush it all day long, possibly pulling on already stressed-out hair.

Okay, so you have tried the rest. Place your brush or comb, shampoo, and conditioner on your altar. Sprinkle fragrant rose petals in a circle around your hair products. Say

242

Aphrodite, Adonis, deities of beauty and love,
Bless this brush with the gentleness of a dove.
By my will and pure desire in the shower,
Infuse this shampoo and conditioner with power.
My hair will grow stronger.
My hair will grow longer.
My hair will grow stronger.
My hair will grow longer.

Repeat this whenever you wash or brush your hair. Saying this incantation over your hair products can even work for a good hair day. Everybody needs an absolutely fabulous hair day once in a while. Maybe it's the day you know your boyfriend or girlfriend is going to break up with you. (How do you know? It seems everyone in your class knows.) Or maybe today is the day you are going to ask your crush to the dance. Maybe you feel lower than dirt and just need a pick-me-up. Regardless, take a moment to relax before you repeat the chant, and really concentrate on your desired outcome. Also, when it is time for a trim, be sure your hair is cut during the new or waning moon.

RELEASE THE TRICKSTER

When I was a teen, I thought my first book would be *1001 Excuses*. I could tell a lie so well that even I believed it. Following my own fabrications became difficult from time to time, as they began to get more and more confused and tangled like a spider's web. There were times when the simplest lie snowballed into a huge deception that backfired something wicked. Using double-talk, lying, or cleverly distracting others to avoid trouble or responsibility is called trickster medicine. The Native Americans call on Coyote or Crow for cunning, the Norse trickster is called Loki, and the English know him as Puck, the mischievous fellow in Shakespeare's *A Midsummer Night's Dream*.

If you fall into this category, you are quite clever. You can make up a lie and make it up quick. You are witty, hardly at a loss for words, and as sharp as a tack; little escapes your bright mind. The trickster is definitely a leader or friend on your path back to Spirit. Think of Wile E. Coyote, super genius. He comes up with the most insane, elaborate trap to catch the speedy roadrunner, but what happens? The trick boomerangs, and he gets run over by the steamroller. The problem is that it is not enough for him. He needs to go back to be sure. "Hey, was that really a steamroller? Did my own trick really come back and bite me in the behind? No, it can't be!" And he is smashed again, flat as a pancake.

Trickster medicine can serve us for a time. We cleverly come up with reasons why Mom's car is out of gas, what happened to our homework, and where we were when the streetlights came on. The mistake you may make, though, is in believing you can go on. All tricksters eventually fool themselves. Someday you may find you have worn the Coyote mask one too many times, and when you look in the mirror, you cannot tell which part is really you and which part is pretend. The key to manipulating this medicine to your benefit is laughter.

Be on the lookout for times you may be fooling yourself. Laugh at yourself. Angels fly because they take themselves so lightly. Release the burdens, and trust. These beginning steps start with fessing up.

Cast this spell during the waxing of the moon, or if it must be done during the waning phase, include a black candle in your ritual to banish hurt feelings. Sunday is a good day for this spell because it symbolizes maintaining relationships, the sun, and bringing the light or truth to the forefront. Light a blue candle for truth, an orange candle for harmony—which will hopefully ensure there is no sacrifice of friendships due to your tricks—and a purple candle for karma. More than likely, you will have some amendment to make, but using a purple candle will help increase your intuition and allow you to foresee a correction that can make the road a little less bumpy. Include in your ritual pictures or images of Loki, Puck, Crow, or Coyote.

Say

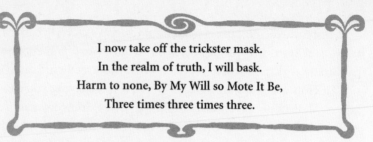

I now take off the trickster mask.
In the realm of truth, I will bask.
Harm to none, By My Will so Mote It Be,
Three times three times three.

Lay the image of the trickster facedown, and repeat the chant.

STOP WORRYING

Worrying is like paying interest on a debt you may not owe. Thought precedes action. When you weigh yourself down with worrisome, debilitating thoughts, it is as if you entered a quagmire. It will not matter how much you struggle to get through; as long as you worry, you will keep sinking deeper. To cast off worrying, meditate.

Turn on meditative or massage music or Buddhist chants. Sit comfortably, light a white, vanilla-scented candle, and place it directly in front of you. You can choose to record the following visual meditation and play it back for yourself or just memorize it.

Close your eyes and visualize yourself in a forest glen. Majestic trees of all forms and shapes surround you. There is a myriad of colors, from the trees' deep and light greens to the sky's cornflower blue and the rich brown of the earth. With each breath, you become calmer and the forest glen becomes clearer and more defined. You may see a forest animal run past. Your angels or other guides may decide to visit. Say hello to your brothers and sisters. Continue to be aware of your breath. Listen to the forest's sounds. You hear a gentle lapping of water. A small pool appears at your feet. Sit beside the water edge, and look for your reflection. Is the water clear and bluish green, or is it murky and brown? Is your brow wrinkled with worry, or are you smiling? If you are smiling and the water looks pure, hold this image and remember that you can be this person always. If the images are gloomy, allow your fingers to skim the surface of the water.

As the rings of water disperse, see a mist forming just under the surface like a tiny tornado. Watch as the mist calmly passes through your image, erasing the lines of despair on your face. A soothing white light rises out of the water and begins to surround you. You are now free from all anxiety, and all the answers will come to you effortlessly and smoothly.

Slowly bring your awareness back to the present by scrunching your toes while still holding the image of yourself embraced by the white light. Watch the white light move through your toes into the earth, flexible enough to travel wherever you go. Allow yourself to feel each part of your body as you come back to the present moment. You are still surrounded by white, cleansing light. Dab vanilla oil behind each ear.

TRAVEL SPELLS

FLY TO THE MOON

The idea that witches can physically fly is a misconception. The rumor originally started when eyewitnesses saw people in ancient times hopping around on their brooms in the middle of the night in some distant field. Most often these nature lovers were jumping with their brooms to show their crops how high they wanted and needed them to grow.

Witches do fly with what is known as astral flight. Astral flight happens when your consciousness floats into the spiritual realms to either meet with other people or see into the future or past. It is similar to dreaming. The herb most associated with astral flight is belladonna. During the Burning Times, witches used the herb to allow their minds to escape the torture to which their bodies were subjected. When a victim was led to the killing device, be it a stake, pyre, or vat of water, they were bombarded by a hissing crowd. Fellow witches hid amongst the persecutors and slipped their friend a bit of belladonna. The accused swallowed the herb and was able to doze her way effortlessly to the other side. Have you ever been in a car accident in which at the moment of impact, you seemed to be elsewhere? It is more than a state of shock. It is a deliberate act to take your awareness out of the nasty situation so your mind does not do further damage than the accident itself.

Cast this spell at midnight. You can even perform the ritual at the same time as a friend whom you want to speak with on the astral plane. Light five white candles, place one in each of the

252

four cardinal directions, and place another one in the center of your pentacle. Burn frankincense incense. You will be invoking Hecate, the Dark Mother, protectress of witches and sender of nighttime visions. She is a powerful goddess who is a representation of the triple aspect of the feminine deity; in other words, she encompasses the Maiden, Mother, and Crone. Place a representation of Hecate on your altar. This can be a picture or statue of her, the Triple Goddess, a horse, boar, and dog (these animals are sacred to her when they are together), or the three phases of the moon. Say

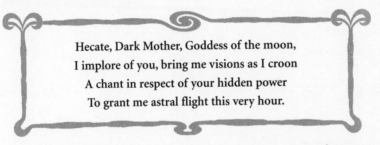

Hecate, Dark Mother, Goddess of the moon,
I implore of you, bring me visions as I croon
A chant in respect of your hidden power
To grant me astral flight this very hour.

Anoint your temples and third eye with sandalwood oil while staring into the flame of your center candle. Clear your mind of everything but the chant.

Visualize yourself drifting out of your body. As you ascend through the roof of your house, or the trees if you are outside, see yourself enclosed by a protective white bubble. Attached to the bubble is a cord that enters your physical body at the belly button and extends to the depths of Mother Earth. This visualization will keep you grounded. Feel the soft breezes of the night sky. Take note of the people, places, and things around you. Stay as long as it feels right. When you hear a voice calling you back to your body, begin your return immediately. Float back through the skies, the trees, the roof, and into your body. See the white light of the bubble descend through your body and into the earth. Write any images or symbols in a dream journal. Also be sure to note your dreams over the next few days.

Visit Faraway Lands

Gypsy wanderlust drifts through the blood of many of us. For some, it's the rarefied air of the Tibetan mountains or the turquoise waters of the Caribbean that call to our souls. For others, it's the open road, the timelessness of traveling through remote lands or visiting cultures and people so foreign to everything we know that it enthralls and appeals.

The first thing to do is explore your own hometown. (Again, we start with the idea of trying everything first on the mundane level to meet the desire). Visit culturally diverse restaurants, culture centers, museums, or libraries. Read up on your favorite places to visit. Visit travel agencies, read the travel section of the newspaper, and talk to your local visitor and convention bureau about helping during their next SATW (Travel Writers) convention—you can assemble press kits, make copies, or organize slides and make a little money, perhaps even a contact or two! If hiking through Costa Rica or going on safari in Uganda is what you crave, buy a good pair of hiking boots or African beads (better yet, ask for them for your next birthday present—you can always try to ask your family members to split the costs of more expensive items). Get a passport. The idea here is to act as if you had the tickets and were leaving next Tuesday. This sends a message of intent to the

Universe. Remember: Believing leads to achieving, and Spirit wants nothing more than for you to be happy and fulfilled.

See if you can befriend someone who might have friends or relatives living in the "old country." On the night of a full moon, clip your fingernails and three strands of hair. Place these items under the light of the full moon. Pull out your hiking boots, a picture of your favorite place, or anything you have gathered that will draw you to the location of your dreams. Close your eyes and take three very deep breaths. Imagine yourself in the perfect spot. See yourself snorkeling, doing yoga, or backpacking—whatever enchants you. Put your hair and nails in an envelope, and sprinkle it with sandalwood oil or powdered sandalwood, or waft sandalwood incense smoke over the envelope. Say

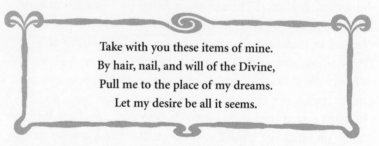

Take with you these items of mine.
By hair, nail, and will of the Divine,
Pull me to the place of my dreams.
Let my desire be all it seems.

Having first asked permission, mail your hair and nails to your friend's contact. You can also ask your new travel agent or travel writer buddy to recommend someone in that country. Ask the person in Tibet, Uganda, or wherever to sprinkle your personal items on Mother Earth or in the ocean. This can also

THE TEEN SPELL BOOK

work if you enclose the hair and nails in a separate envelope; just ask them to bury the envelope. Alternatively, you can put your charmed hair and clippings in the suitcase of someone who is traveling to your favorite location. Bon voyage!

GLOSSARY

Affirmation A positive, repetitive declaration about something you want to manifest in your life. It always needs to be in the positive and present form.

Altar A table, stand, platform, etc. that holds sacred objects in dedication to the One Creator/Spirit and a host of gods and goddesses.

Amulet A consecrated piece of jewelry or coin that is often worn or carried, which has been instilled with special desires such as prosperity or inspiration, although it will often include protection.

Anoint To rub oil on something for ceremonial or magickal purposes.

Archetype An original, deep-seated image or model commonly believed to be the perfect example or representation of a group or type.

Astrology The art-science of identifying and clarifying the basic personality traits of a person through reference to planetary movement and position.

Aura The magnetic force field surrounding a human being, which can be seen or photographed as pulsating and floating colors. The colors reveal one's state of mind.

Banish To assertively drive energy away from a specific area or yourself.

Book of Shadows Also known as a grimoire, it is a diary or journal of rituals, spells, and traditional lore.

Censer A heatproof container, usually a metal bowl or covered incense holder, for burning herbs, incense, or resin used to smudge a circle or in performing magick.

Chakra	Energy centers or vortexes located throughout body.
Charge	To infuse an object with personal power.
Clairvoyant	One who has the ability to foresee or intuit events.
Cone of Power	A method of directing the energy of an individual or group for a singular purpose or to provide a connection to Spirit.
Consecrate	The act of cleansing and blessing an item, most often for magickal or spiritual purposes. May also include infusing or filling a focused intent into the item.
Deosil	Clockwise, or going with the sun's direction. Used to gather, build, and strengthen positive energy.
Divination	The art or practice of foretelling or predicting the future under the influence of Spirit.
Dowsing Rod	Usually made out of wood, this tool (shaped like an upside-down "Y") is often used to find water as well as for divination.
Dragon's Blood	This is an actual tropical plant and/or tree. Although it possesses particularly strong magickal powers, it is also used for coloring varnishes and in photoengraving. It derived its name from the gum resin, which is reddish-brown, similar to dried blood, and the Latin name is *Calamus draco,* which has been named after the constellation Draco the Dragon in the Northern Hemisphere.
Elements	The four fundamental substances (air, fire, water, and earth) that constitute physical matter. Also known as the four points of reference of consciousness.
Energy	The celestial or primal force that is individually generated and can be combined with others for greater strength (as in a cone of power).

Esbat	A Wiccan ritual, usually performed on a full or new moon.
Ether	The transient substance swirling throughout all spaces.
Eye of Newt	The Newt refers to a mythological creature and is related to the salamander. The incorporation of the eye refers to vision. Therefore this term means to receive supernatural foresight. It was popularized by Shakespeare's writings.
Grounding	The act of releasing unwanted energy and centering or aligning oneself with the balance of nature and Spirit.
Image Candle	A candle infused with your unmatched energy, personality, and power.
Incantation	A chant with the intention of bringing magick into your life.
Intuition	To look in, consider, and respect the truth within yourself.
Invoke	To call forth energy from your angels, guides, God, Goddess, and other spiritual beings.
Karma	The universal law and order of cause and effect, which demonstrates that whatever you do will come back to you.
Magick	The art of getting desired results.
Meditation	An exercise requiring an emphasis on breathing and relaxing the mind's chatter for purposes of harmonizing and balancing oneself.
Metaphysical	Events that occur beyond physical explanation.
Oracle	A person of great knowledge who speaks the wisdom of Spirit.
Otherworld	The world where spirits abide, waiting to be reborn.

THE TEEN SPELL BOOK

Paganism	Nature-based religion. The word *pagan* derives from the Latin word *paganus,* which means peasant and *pagus,* which translates to country. Therefore, the resulting word means a country or rustic person.
Pantheon	Collection or group of gods and goddesses in a specific mythical or religious structure.
Pentacle	A physical representation of a pentagram.
Pentagram	A five-pointed star symbolizing the four elements in balance with Spirit.
Rede	An advised plan of conduct and ethics.
Reincarnation	The belief that life and death are a cycle. After you leave this life, you spend time with Spirit until you are reborn, to experience various situations and perspectives
Ritual	A sacred system of ceremonial acts in observance and accordance of one's spirituality.
Runes	An ancient alphabet inscribed on stones for the purpose of bringing in Spirit.
Sabbat	One of eight festivals that celebrate earth, God, Goddess, and the ever-changing cycle of the seasons.
Sacred Space	A hallowed or blessed area that has been cleansed and prepared for magickal purposes.
Smudging	A ritual used whenever or wherever you feel the need to cleanse, balance, protect, or purify yourself, others, a room, your crystals, or other special tools, using the smoke from an embering bundle of sage.
Spell	A means of helping one channel or direct wishes and desires from the spiritual realm to the material.
Spirit	The ever-present life spark that exists as the One Great Creator and the Divine light in every being and thing.
Supernatural	Events and experiences occurring beyond the natural

order of things. Also, unexplainable events and experiences attributed to the spiritual realm.

Talisman A consecrated item that brings good luck, averts evil, and embodies your personal magick.

Tarot A set of playing cards used to perceive the past, foretell the future, or divine current possible pathways.

Totem An animal symbol or spirit that guides one throughout life.

Underworld The opposite side of the living. According to mythology, the Underworld was formally earth but then came under the rule of Hades, the Greek god of the dead.

Visualization The act of using your mind to "see" events outside your physically visual perception.

Wicca A nature-based religion derived from the Anglo-Saxon root word *wicce,* meaning "to bend or shape" as well as "wise."

Widdershins Counterclockwise, or going against the sun's direction. Used to banish, wither, or remove unwanted energy.

Wortcunning The art of growing and using herbs for magickal and healing purposes.

Zodiac The visible path of the planets, sun, and moon around the earth; the twelve signs.

RESOURCE GUIDE
MAGICKAL AND METAPHYSICAL SHOPS

The following shops carry the best selection of books, tarot cards, crystals, herbs, bells, clothing, ritual items, Wiccan tools, and more. Some offer classes, workshops, or gatherings. For additional shops in your area check out www.witchvox.com.

Alabama
Lodestar Books
2827 Highland Avenue
Birmingham, AL 35205
(205) 328-0144
www.lodestarbooks.com

Alaska
The Source—Metaphysical Books and Supplies
329 East 5th Avenue
Anchorage, AK 99501
(907) 274-5850

Arkansas
Mystic Encounters
1630 S. Eight Street #1
Rogers, AR 72756
(501) 621-5910
www.1xpress.com/mystic

Arizona
A Magickal Moon
113 East Southern Avenue
Tempe, AZ 85282
(480) 303-8368

Center for the New Age
341 Highway 179
Sedona, AZ 86336
(520) 282-2085

California

Ancient Ways
4075 Telegraph Avenue
Oakland, CA 94609
(510) 653-3244
www.ancientways.com

Assembly of Wiccan Bookstore
4715 Franklin Blvd.
Sacramento, CA 95820
(916) 455-0109

Points of Light
4358 Sterns St.
Long Beach, CA 90815
(562) 985-3388

Starcrafts
1909 Cable Street
San Diego, CA 92107
(619) 224-4923
www.starcraftsob.com

Colorado

Alternate Realities
3170 East Fourth Avenue
Durango, CO 81301
(970) 247-3260

Metamorphosis /SpiritWise
6590 South Broadway
Littleton, CO 80121
(303) 730-2974

Connecticut

Curious Goods Witchcraft Shop
415 Campbell Ave.
West Haven, CT 06516
(203) 932-1193
curiousgds@aol.com

Delaware

Trinket's—The Magickal Kat
2-A Baltimore Avenue
Rehoboth Beach, DE 19971
(302) 226-2466

Florida

WHVH Book Shop
4578 St. John's Avenue
Jacksonville, FL 32210
(904) 387-2064

J & D Visions
14095 W. Dixie Hwy. #113
Miami, FL 33161
(305) 792-4621
www.jdvisions.bigstep.com

New Age Books and Things
4401 North Federal Highway
Fort Lauderdale, FL 33308
(954) 771-0026
www.newagebooksandthings.com

Georgia

Crystal Blue
1168 Euclid Avenue NE
Atlanta, GA 30307
(404) 522-4605

Hawaii

Sedona
Ward Centre
1200 Ala Moana Blvd.
Honolulu, HI 96814
(808) 591-8010
www.sedona_hi.com

Idaho

The Purple Moon Crystal Co.
50 East Main
P.O. Box 549
Lava Hot Springs, ID 83246
(208) 776-5475
www.purplemooncrystal.com
Pmooncrystal@aol.com

Illinois

Minor Arcana
1852 Damen Avenue
Chicago, IL 60647
(773) 252-1389
www.minorarcana.com

New Ages/Other Worlds
1337 Walnut Street
Murphysboro, IL 62966
(618) 687-5135
www.newagesotherworlds.net-firm.com

Indiana

World of Wisdom
5142 Madison Avenue Ste. 4
Indianapolis, IN 46227
(317) 787-3005

Crescent Moon
3808 Highway 62
Jeffersonville, IN 47130
(812) 256-0247

Iowa

Crescent Moon
1800 Central Avenue
Dubuque, IA 52001
(319) 495-0390

Kansas

Enchanted Willow Alchemy Shoppe
418 SW 6th Avenue
Topeka, KS 66603-3110
(785) 235-3776
www.enchantedwillow.com

Kentucky

White Raven
609 Main Street
Covington, KY 41011
(859) 291-5178

The Copper Cauldron
3016 US 60 East
Owensboro, KY 42303
(270) 683-4100
www.copper-cauldron.com

Louisiana

Esoterica Occult Goods
541 Rue Dumaine Street
New Orleans, LA 70116
(800) 353-7001
mail@onewitch.com
www.onewitch.com

Maine

Crystal Crescents
103 Congress Street
Rumford, ME 04276
(207) 364-4600
www.crystalcrescent.netfirms

Maryland

Bell, Book, and Candle
7684 Bel Air Road
Baltimore, MD 21236
www.bellbookandcandle.com

Massachusetts

The Broom Closet
3 Central Street
Salem, MA 01970
(978) 741-3669
www.broomcloset.com

Some Enchanted Evening
13-A Mechanic Street
Spencer, MA 01562
(508) 885-2050

Michigan

*Crazy Wisdom Bookstore
and Tea Room*
114 S. Main Street
Ann Arbor, MI 48104
(734) 665-2757
www.crazywisdom.net

Isle of Avalon Books
412 East Fourth Street
Royal Oak, MI 48067
(800) 306-5811
www.isleofavalonbooks.com

Minnesota

Magus Books and Herbs
13165 East Fourth Street
Minneapolis, MN 55414
(800) 99MAGNUS
www.magusbooks.com

Mississippi

Silver Moon Shop
3709 Beachview Drive Ste. C
Ocean Springs, MS 39564
(228) 872-0506

Missouri

Ancient Wisdom
719 East Church Street
Aurora, MO 65605
(866) 891-3785
http://awmarker.com
/AncientWisdom

Mystic Valley
3228 Laclede Station Road
St. Louis, MO 63310
(314) 645-3336
www.mysticvalley.com

Montana

Nature's Pantry
318 Central Avenue
Great Falls, MT 59406
(406) 268-1233

Nebraska

The Next Millennium
2308 North 72nd Street
Omaha, NE 68134
(402) 393-1121
www.next-mill.com

Nevada

Bell, Book and Candle
1725 East Charleston Blvd., Ste. C
Las Vegas, NV 89104
(702) 386-2950

New Hampshire

Ancient Moon
107 West Pearl Street
Nashua, NH 03060
(603) 882-8013

New Jersey

Equinox Books &
Occult Supplies
108 Brighton Avenue
Long Branch, NJ 07740
(732) 222-0801
www.monmouth.com
/~equinoxbook/index.html

New Mexico

Moonrise Books
2617-D Juan Tato NE
Albuquerque, NM 87112
(505) 332-2665
www.moonrisebooks.com

New York

The Grove
262 East 14th Street
Elmira Heights, NY 14903
(607) 733-8964
www.grovebookstore.com

Morgana's Chamber
242 West 10th Street
New York, NY 10014
(212) 243-3415

The Psychic's Thyme
16 Edmonds Street
Rochester, NY 14607
(716) 473-4230
psikic101@yahoo.com
psychicsthyme@yahoo.com

North Carolina
Crystal Connection
5725 Oleander Drive, Bldg. F1 Ste 2
Wilmington, NC 28430
(910) 796-1433

World Junkets
704 Brookstown Avenue
Winston-Salem, NC 27101
(336) 722-0105

North Dakota
Star Lightrider's Curious Goods
121 Eighth Street South
Morehead, ND 58102
(701) 232-2221
starladyr@aol.com
www.lightriders.safeshopper.com

Ohio
The Mystic Goddess
453 East Exchange Street
Akron, OH 44304
(330) 762-5550
www.mysticgoddess.com

The Occult Shop
3647 West Eighth Street
Cincinnati, OH 45205
(313) 471-5200
http://occultshop.safeshopper.com

Oklahoma
Explore . . . Mind, Body, Spirit
4417 North Western
Oklahoma City, OK 73118
(405) 524-6700

Oregon
Moonshadow
3352 SE Hawthorne Blvd.
Portland, OR 97214
(503) 235-5774

Mrs. Thompson's Herbs, Gifts and Folklore
1145 Lincoln Street
Eugene, OR 97401
(541) 686-6136
www.celtic.net

Pennsylvania

Moonstones... A Metaphysical Shop
1517 Potomac
Pittsburgh, PA 15228
(412) 343-4444
www.moonhaven.com

Hand of Aries II/Morgan's Cauldron
509 South Sixth Street
Philadelphia, PA 19147
(215) 923-5264
www.handofaries2.com

Rhode Island

The Mind's Eye
182 Thames Street
Newport, RI 02840
(401) 849-7333

South Carolina

The Dragon's Treasure
1922 Cedar Lane Road
Greenville, SC 29617
(864) 294-0094
www.thedragonstreasure.com

Green Dragon
7671 Northwoods Blvd., Ste. T
North Charleston, SC 29406
(843) 797-2052
www.thegreendragon.org

Tennessee

The Goddess and the Moon
512 Heather Place
Nashville, TN 37204
(615) 383-3039

Violet Moon
521 North Main Street
Greenville, TN 37745
(423) 638-4589

Texas

Natural Magic
5209 Martin Avenue
Austin, TX 78751
(512) 451-4491
www.naturalmagic.cx

The Enchanted Forest Metaphysical Shoppe
6619 East Lancaster Avenue
Fort Worth, TX 76112
(817) 446-8388

Mystik Rainbow
1813 61st Street
Galveston, TX 77551
(409) 744-8106

Utah

Gypsy Moon Emporium
1011 East 900 South
Salt Lake City, UT 84105
(801) 521-9100
www.dorsnet.com/~gypsymn/

Vermont
Queen of Pentacles
32 State Street
Montpelier, VT 05602
(802) 223-8972

Virginia
Mystic Moon
3416 North Military Highway
Norfolk, VA 25318
(757) 855-3280

Divine Magic & Novelties
5943 Midlothian Turnpike
Richmond, VA 23224
(804) 232-1345

Washington
Open Door Bookstore
1604 North Monroe Street
Spokane, WA 99208
(509) 328-8283

Gypsy Lily's Caravan of Dreams
2713 Sixth Avenue
Tacoma, WA 98407
(253) 428-0273

West Virginia
Oasis of the Spirit
2255 Market Street
Wheeling, WV 26003
(304) 232-5768

Wisconsin
Magical Delights
605 Third Street
Wausau, WI 54401
(715) 848-1982
Mystic Dreams
40 North Johnston Street
Hartford, WI 53027
(262) 670-0142

Wyoming
Crystal Clear
342 East "K"
Casper, WY 82601
(307) 266-4742

THE TEEN SPELL BOOK

CANADA

Alberta
Where Faeries Live
10991a 124 Street
Edmonton, Alberta
T5M OH9
(780) 454-0187
www.planet.eon.net/~bron-
wynn/WhereFaeriesLive_com.html

British Columbia
Aunt Agatha's Occult Emporium
46 Begbie Street,
New Westminister, British
Columbia
V31 3M9
(604) 516-6959
http://web.idirect.com/~agatha

New Brunswick
Tranquility Book & Gift Ltd.
1111Regent St. Unit 13,
Fredericton, New Brunswick
E3B 3Z2
(506) 450-7915

Nova Scotia
Little Mysteries Books
1663 Barrington Street
Halifax, Nova Scotia
B3J 1Z0
(902) 423-1313
www.littlemysteries.com

Ontario
The Ancient Earth
314 St Paul Street
St. Catherines, Ontario
L2R 3M9
(905) 688-0111

Quebec
*The Magical Blend Metaphysical
Books and Gifts*
1928 St. Catherine Street West
Montreal, Quebec
H3H 1MA
(514) 939-1458
www.themagicalblend.com

Saskatchewan
*Witches Brew Metaphysical Books
and Gifts*
126-20th Street West
Saskatoon, Saskatchewan
S7M 0W6
(306) 665-6612

AUSTRALIA

Queensland
The Wizard's Realm
Shop 25, 3-15 Orchid Avenue
Surfers Paradise, Queensland 4217
(07) 5538 3445
www.wizardsrealm.com.au/

Western Australia
The Cauldron
Shop 8/306 Great Eastern Highway
Midland
Perth, Western Australia 6056
(08) 9274 8900

New South Wales
Ceridwen's Cauldron
Shop 3, 16 Nelson Street
Fairfield, New South Wales 2165
(02) 9755 7199

MAIL ORDER CATALOGS

Amber Lotus Publishing
537 Castro Street
San Francisco, CA 94114
(800) 326-2375
www.amberlotus.com
Illuminating Spirit in the world
with beautifully designed calendars. Call or e-mail for your free
catalog.

Azure Green
48 Chester Road, Dept. WIG
Chester, MA 01011
(413) 623-2155
www.azuregreen.com
Amulets, jewelry, herbs, incense,
perfumes, censers, candles, statues,
and other ritual items. Call or
write for a free catalog.

Ancient Circles
PO Box 610
Laytonville, CA 95451
(800) 726-8032
Celtic jewelry, Goddess and God
pendants, temple formula perfumes, and more. Send $2 for the
catalog.

The Bead Tree
PO Box 682
West Falmouth, MA 02574
(508) 548-4665
Goddess earrings and pendants, as
well as symbols of air, fire, water,
and earth. Send $1 for the catalog.

Bountiful Creations-Wellness
Specialists
PO Box 750236
Forest Hills, NY 11432
(718) 739-7051
www.bountifulcreations.com
Specializes in natural remedies and
products such as altar cloths,
candles, lotions, herbs, natural oils,
ritual wear, astrological charts,
herbal remedies, and workshop
and online classes. All items are
reusable or refillable. Send $2 for
the catalog (refundable with first
purchase).

Creatrix
PO Box 56
West Hurley, NY 12491
www.melissaharris.com/creatrix
Visionary images of Goddess
celebration on cards, prints,
magnets, T-shirts, and journals.
Send $3 for a brochure (credited
on first order).

DragonStar T-shirts
Bright Blessings
PO Box 464
Dallas, TX 30132
www.bright-blessings.com
Beautifully designed T-shirts
featuring Wheel of the Year, Green
Man, Gaia, Celtic cross and more.
Send for a free color brochure.

The Excelsior Incense Works
1413 Van Dyke Avenue
San Francisco, CA 94124
(415) 822-9124
Incense from around the world,
religious statues from India, raw
materials to make incense, crystals,
and candles. Send $1 for the
catalog.

Gaia Gal Productions
2027 Sixth Avenue South
Great Falls, MN 59405
Gaiagal135@hotmail.com
Clay goddess images and goddess
stickers.

Gypsy Heaven
115 S. Main Street
New Hope, PA 18938
(215) 862-5251
"The Witch Shop of New Hope!"
Specializes in cauldrons, mortar
and pestles, jewelry, books, herbs,
oils, incense, and more. Send $3
for a catalog.

Ladyslipper, Inc.
PO Box 3124
Durham, NC 27715
(800) 634-6044
New Age, Celtic, Native American,
and drumming music, as well as
pagan notecards and calendars.
Free catalog.

Lavender Folk Herbal
PO Box 1261 Dept. SW
Boulder, CO 80306
Handmade medicinal and
magickal tea blends. Send $2
for the catalog.

**Llewellyn's New Worlds of Mind
and Spirit**
(800) The-moon
Books, horoscopes, weather and
earthquake forecasts, and New Age
items. Call for a free issue.

**Pyramid Books and the New Age
Collection**
PO Box 48
35 Congress Street
Salem, MA 01970
(508) 744-6261
This extensive catalog offers
clothes, books, ritual and New Age
items, and music. Send $1 for the
catalog.

Sacred Source
PO Box SW
Crozer, VA 22932
(800) 290-6203
www.sacredsource.com
"Ancient images, Ancient
Wisdom." Offers Goddess statues,
prints, drums, music, books,
jewelry, and more.

Songs for Earthlings
Emerald Earth Publishing
PO Box 4326
Philadelphia, PA 19118
(888) 333-3929
www.emeradearth.net
A Green spirituality songbook
with over 400 songs and chants
that honor the Earth and all Her
inhabitants, with songs on food
blessings, lullabies, life passages,
getting along, taking care of each
other, and more.

Triskele Pagan Supply
295 Blight Street
Miami
Canada
R0G 1H0
(204) 435-2500
http://triskele.hypermart.net
Bath salts and accessories,
handmade to order. Check the
Web site or request a catalog.

WEB SITES

www.delphi.com/walkinlove
This Teen Witch forum is quite
busy, and runs contests, a weekly
e-zine, as well as good old-fashioned
fun chats.

www.espirituality.com
Up-to-date information on
spirituality, empowerment,
spiritual teachers, psychology,
astrology, fitness, health, and
wellness.

www.e-witch.com
A Pagan auction site for all
magickal items.

www.eyeofthecat.com
This site and store boasts one of
the best selections of magickal
herbs around as well as terrific
Wicca and magickal classes. Store
is located in Long Beach, CA.

www.goddessdesigns.com
Terrific spiritual and ethnic stencils
for the creative spirit within you.

www.isisbooks.com
For over twenty years this store
(located in Colorado) has offered
books, incense, statues, Feng Shui
supplies, Tarot cards, jewelry,
herbs, essential oils, and more.

www.krystalmoon.com
Krystal Moon can supply you with everything you've read about in this book: candles, oils, herbs and more. If they don't carry it, they will find it for you. Store location is 21168 Beach, Blvd, Huntington Beach, CA. 92648. Phone: 714-960-8798. Best of all they will do their best to keep it affordable for just about every budget. The owners are Wiccan who practice the White side of Magick and understand your needs.

www.magikalwishingwell.com
Magikal Wishing Well is a place for all of your metaphysical needs. They honor other people's beliefs and support their expression of those beliefs. The shop was created to put you in contact with products that will enhance and support your spirituality. They carry candles and incense, books and ritual tools, tarot and accessories, herbs and aromatherapy, and custom-made jewelry. The store is located in Tacoma, Washington.

www.pointsoflight.com
Wildcrafted herbs, oils, handmade incense, capes, statues, books, athames, stones, tarot cards, and

more. The store is located in Long Beach, California.

www.prolificpagans.com
A Web resource for the latest in pagan reading and author news.

www.psychiceyebookshops.com
The largest chain of metaphysical stores located in California and Nevada. Stores and online stores carry oils, books, candles, incense, altar items, and more.

www.realm-of-shade.com/spiritcraft
Ritual Robes, cauldrons, celestial bags, talisman bags, tarot bags, incense, bath salts, instruments, jewelry, charm bags, besoms, discs, chalices, steel torches, rune sets, pendulums, goddess charms, pan horns, elemental pentacles, handmade charcoal incense discs, masks, scrying mirrors, magick quill pens, grimoires, marble pentacles, wood-burned natal charts, and more.

www.roseandchalice.com
Roseandchalice.com carries an extensive assortment of altar cloths, figure candles, aromatherapy candles, astrology charts, blades, swords, divination tools, tarot decks, runes, jewelry, pewter

chalices and goblets, Tibetan singing bowls, phurbas, prayer bells, and more. They also offer 100% beeswax candles, mystical fragrance oils, bath salts, incense, mystical inks, and quill pens. All items are handcrafted in accordance with the ancient traditions and produced within a sacred circle during the proper moon phase and time to instill them with the best possible vibrations for your enjoyment and spiritual journey.

www.snapdragongifts.com
Jewelry, holiday cards, sculpture, incense, oils, candles, T-shirts, stickers, puzzles and toys, medieval products, and more.

www.soapgoddess.com
A handmade soap company offering soaps made with magick.

www.spiralscouts.org
Spiral Scouts provides an opportunity for pagan children to interact with each other. Sprial Scouts strives to instill in our children the concepts of inclusivity, the balance of gender energies, and tolerance for differences of belief. The pagan worldview as well as personal growth and development are encouraged.

teaandsympathy.com
This site offers an extensive selection of Scottish, English, and Welsh books, including many on history and genealogy, as well as Celtic jewelry, Highland Games information, and imported gifts.

www.witchonthego.com
Magickal tools for busy people, including spell and ritual kits, handcrafted spell candles, fine ritual incense, custom-designed rituals, and Wiccan information.

www.witchvox.com
The premier Wiccan resource Web site for all the information you could want on earth-based spirituality, Wicca, the sabbats, and more. Includes additional store information and a Wiccan teen chat room!

PERIODICALS

The Beltane Papers
A Journal of Women's Mysteries
PO Box 29694-SW
Bellingham, WA 98228-1694
www.thebeltanepapers.net
Specializing in beautiful artwork, feminist articles, folklore, mythology, music, recipes, reviews, crafts, and herb and Goddess lore. Accepts submissions from artists and writers. A sample issue is $5 within the US and $7 elsewhere.

The Blessed Bee
P.O. Box 641
Point Arena, CA 95468
(707) 882-2052
www.blessedbee.com
This is a pagan, family-oriented, quarterly magazine full of resources, stories, and networking. A one-year subscription is $13 ($17 elsewhere). Call for free sample.

Circle Network News
Circle Sanctuary
PO Box 219
Mt. Horeb, WI 53517
(608) 924-2216
www.circlesanctuary.org

Since 1978 this quarterly magazine has been serving Wiccans, pagans, and other nature folk. Circle Sanctuary offers information on Wiccans Ways, shamanism, nature spirituality, rituals, sacred sites, traditions, readers' forum, news, and contacts. A one-year subscription is $25 via bulk mail, $34 first class mail and Canada, and $38 outside the USA. Sample issue is $5. Free brochure.

Covenant of the Goddess
Newsletter
Covenant of the Goddess
PO Box 17
Blue Mound, WI 53517
www.cog.org
Announcements, articles, and resources of interest to Witches, and COG news and business. Published eight times a year.

Earth First! Journal
PO Box 3023
Tucson, AZ 85702
(520) 620-6900
www.earthfirstjournal.com
Radical and deep ecology articles as well as wilderness preservation

and biological diverse articles. Published on the eight nature holidays. A one-year subscription is $25.

Green Egg Magazine
212 South Main Street #22B
Willits, CA 95490
(707) 456-0332
www.greenegg.org
One of the premier pagan magazines, *Green Egg* features articles, art, interfaith dialogues, columns, fiction, humor, events calendar, folklore, shamanism, green activism, and poetry. A one-year subscription is $28 a year via bulk mail, $42 a year first-class mail and Canada, and $63 outside the USA. Sample issue is $5.

The Messenger
PO Box 1971
Glendora, CA 91740
(626) 335-0428
www.themessenger.cc
The Messenger focuses on New Age, metaphysical, spiritual, and alternative health issues, and self-empowerment. Regular columns include palmistry, astrology, numerology, NLP, and Dear Louise (by Louise Hay). A one-year subscription to this monthly magazine is $20.

New Moon Magazine
PO Box 3620
Duluth, MN 55803
(800) 381-4743
newmoon@newmoon.org
www.newmoon.org
Targeted at girls 8–14, New Moon Publishing produces media for every girl who wants her voice heard and her dreams taken seriously, and for every adult who cares about girls.

Of Like Mind
Box 6677
Madison, WI 53716
(608) 244-0072
Published since 1983, this newspaper focuses on women's spirituality, Goddess religion, Paganism, earth connection, and native and nature paths. A one-year subscription is $15–35, based on a sliding scale. A sample issue is $4.

Pan Gaia
PO Box 641
Point Arena, CA 95468
(707) 882-2052
www.pangaia.com
Earth-wise spirituality magazine geared for both men and women. Focuses on a proactive worldly approach of bringing paganism down-to-earth. It is the yang

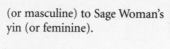

(or masculine) to Sage Woman's yin (or feminine).

Sage Woman
PO Box 641
Point Arena, CA 95468-0641
(707) 882-2052
www.sagewoman.com
This incredible magazine honors "the Goddess in Every Woman." Each issue focuses on a central theme and includes Goddess lore, feature articles, magic, astrology, herbs, a readers' forum, and reviews of books and music.

The Seeker Journal
PO Box 3326
Ann Arbor, MI 48106
This newsletter seeks to offer unique experiences and knowledge among followers of esoteric and mystical traditions.

Starlight Voices
c/o Linda Clark
PO Box 421495
Los Angeles CA 90042
1-877-585-5308 EXT 497 or
1-877-708-7845 EXT 558
www.members.tripod.com/~starlightvoices
Starlightvoices@hotmail.com
Starlight Voices is a newsletter for young pagans. Its purpose is to provide a safe and informational guide for young pagans to learn from and enjoy. Its goal is to provide a service that will bring about more awareness of the earth spirituality that is in the young pagans of today.

The Unicorn
PO Box 0691
Kirkland, WA 98083-0691
www.therowantreechurch.org
In operation since 1976, The Unicorn newsletter offers eight issues a year each filled with poetry, artwork, and articles celebrating the Sabbats, plus books reviews, stories, and news! A one-year subscription is $13.00/year in North America, $17.00 elsewhere

Yoga Journal
2054 University Avenue, Ste. 600
Berkeley, CA 94707
(510) 841-9200
www.yogajournal.com
This magazine focuses on the practice and daily application of yoga principles, with regular features such as well-being, body & spirit, awakened athlete, and much more. A one-year subscription is $17.

280

RECOMMENDED READING

Adler, Margot. *Drawing Down the Moon.* New York: Penguin, 1979.

Aswynn, Freya. *Northern Mysteries and Magick: Runes, Gods, and Feminine Powers.* St. Paul, MN: Llewellyn, 1998.

Bethards, Betty. *The Dream Book: Symbols for Self-Understanding.* Rockport, MA: Element, 1995.

Buckland, Raymond. *Buckland's Complete Book of Witchcraft.* St. Paul, MN: Llewellyn, 1986.

Budapest, Zsuzsanna E. *The Grandmother of Time.* San Francisco: Harper and Row, 1989.

Campbell, Joseph. *Myths to Live By.* New York: Bantam Books, 1972.

Conway, D.J. *A Little Book of Altar Magic.* Freedom, CA: The Crossing Press, 2000.

Cunningham, Scott. *Cunningham's Encyclopedia of Magical Herbs.* St. Paul, MN: Llewellyn, 1985.

_____. *Wicca: A Guide for the Solitary Practitioner.* St. Paul, MN: Llewellyn, 1985.

Dunwich, Gerina. *Wicca Craft: The Modern Witch's Book of Herbs, Magick, and Dreams.* Secaucus, NJ: Citadel Press Book, 1997.

_____. *The Wicca Sourcebook.* Secaucus, NJ: Citadel Press Book, 1997.

Farrar, Janet, and Stewart Farrar. *The Witches' Goddesses.* Washington, DC: Phoenix, 1987

_____. *The Witches' Gods.* Washington, DC: Phoenix, 1987

Forrest, Steven. *The Inner Sky.* San Diego, CA: ASC Publishing, 1989.

Gawain, Shakti. *Creative Visualization.* New York: Bantam, 1983.

Gibran, Khalil. *The Prophet.* New York: Knopf, 1969.

Graves, Robert. *The White Goddess.* New York: Farrar, Straus and Giroux, 1948.

Grimassi, Raven. *Italian Witchcraft: The Old Religion of Southern Europe.* St. Paul, MN: Llewellyn, 2000.

_____. *Ways of the Strega, Italian Witchcraft: Its Lore, Magick and Spells.* St. Paul, MN: Llewellyn, 1995.

Harris, Eleanor L. *Ancient Egyptian Divination and Magic.* York Beach, ME: Samuel Weiser Publishing, 1998.

Hay, Louise. *You Can Heal Your Life.* Carson, CA: Hay House, 1984.

Judith, Anodea. *Wheels of Life: A User's Guide to the Chakra System.* St. Paul, MN: Llewellyn, 1994.

Jung, Carl. *Man and His Symbols.* Garden City, NY: Doubleday, 1964.

Kruger, Anna. *An Illustrated Guide to Herbs, Their Medicine and Magic.* Surrey, UK: Dragon's World, 1993.

McCoy, Edain. *The Sabbats: A New Approach to Living the Old Ways.* St. Paul, MN: Llewellyn, 1994.

Melody, A. *Love Is in the Earth: A Kaleidoscope of Crystals.* Wheat Ridge, CO: Earth Love Publishing House, 1995.

Monroe, Douglas. *The 21 Lessons of Merlyn: A Study in Druid Magic & Lore.* St. Paul, MN: Llewellyn, 1994.

Moura, Ann. *Origins of Modern Witchcraft: The Evolution of a World Religion.* St. Paul, MN: Llewellyn, 2000.

Mynne, Hugh. *The Faerie Way.* St. Paul, MN: Llewellyn, 1998.

Rathbun, Ron. *The Way Is Within.* New York: Berkeley Publishing, 1997.

Roberts, Morgan. *The Norse Gods and Heroes.* New York: Metro Books, 1995.

Samms, Jamie and David Carson. *Medicine Cards.* Santa Fe, NM: Bear & Co., 1988.

Sark. *A Creative Companion: How to Free Your Creative Spirit.* Berkeley, CA: Celestial Arts, 1991.

Starhawk. *Spiral Dance: A Rebirth of the Ancient Religion of the Great Goddess.* San Francisco: Harper San Francisco, 1979.

Starhawk, Diane Baker and Anne Hill. *Circle Round: Raising Children in Goddess Traditions.* New York: Bantam, 1998.

Taylor, Terry Lynn. *Messenger of the Light: The Angel's Guide to Spiritual Growth.* Tiburon, CA: HJ Kraemer, Inc., 1995.

Waldner, Kris. *The Book of Goddesses.* Hillsboro, OR: Beyond Words Publishing, 1995.

Weiss, Gaea and Shandor. *Growing and Using the Healing Herbs.* Emmaus, PA: Wings Books, 1985.

INDEX

THE TEEN SPELL BOOK

Trust
  by parents, spell for, 140–142
  regaining, spell for, 240–241
  in your instincts, 118
Tuaret (goddess), 43
Turquoise, significance of, 174

U

Ukko (god), 33
Understanding from others, spell to get,
  88–90
Underworld, 262
Unseen forces, shaping or bending, 17

V

Venus (goddess), 36
  spells involving, 149–150, 238–239
Verbal abuse, spell against, 86–87
Vesta (goddess), 34
Violets, significance of, 142
Virgin Mary (goddess), 32
Visualization, 61, 194, 262
Voice inside, 1–3, 118

W

Wardrobe, spell for, 238–239
Ways, The, 13–14
Weaknesses, spell to accept, 226–227
West (Direction), 67, 74
Wicca
  books and magazines about, 277–283
  definition of, 5, 262
  relationship with other religions, 17
  solitary practice of, 15
  talking with others about, 19–21
  See also Spells
Wiccan code words, 8
Wiccan holidays, 23–28
  deities of, 29–45
Wiccan Redes, 10, 29
Wiccan symbols, 81
  animal totems, 52–53, 126–127

colors, 77–78
days of the week, 79
Four Directions, 72–74
months of the year, 76–77
moon, 75–76
pentacle, 180–181, 222–223
pentagram, 72, 261
runes, 14–15, 55–59
See also names of specific herbs, flowers,
  gemstones, and oils
Wiccan traditions, 10–16
Wiccan view of death, 24
Widdershins, 262
Winning, spells for, 216–217, 234–235
Winter Solstice, 24
  goddesses and gods of, 32–33
Wishes, making, 69
Witches
  flying, 252–254
  origins of the word, 16
  trials and burnings of, 6–10
  who are they?, 17–19
Wodin (god), 14, 32
Words, the power of, 95
Work, spells to find, 128–131, 206–207
Worrying, spell to stop, 247–248
Wortcunning, 262

X

Xiuhtecutli (god), 42
Xochipilli (god), 37, 43
Xochiquetzal (goddess), 39

Y

Yachimata-Hiko (god), 33
Yemana (goddess), 32

Z

Zeus (god), 42
Zodiac, 262
Zoe (goddess), 41
Zorya Vechernaya (goddess), 31